Mountaineering Tourism

This book offers a critical account of the historical evolution of mountaineering and its relation to the phenomenon of tourism, providing an overview of recent developments linked to the diversification, commodification, and commercialisation of mountaineering activity.

Mountaineering, broadly defined as hiking, trekking, and climbing, is now a mass phenomenon, with continually growing numbers of trekkers, climbers, and religious tourists hiking in mountain regions. Increasing visitor numbers require the current policies to be updated. The environments around high-mountain areas and their local resident communities, until recently cut off from civilisation, are sensitive to outside influences and have been abruptly exposed to the impact of mountaineering and related activities. This is the first book to disentangle overlapping terms and definitions related to mountaineering tourism. It identifies the key terms and turning points in mountaineering tourism and discusses the impacts of mountaineering tourism from an environmental, sociocultural, and personal perspective and identifies current tourism management policies. Finally, this book provides a continuum between the past and future of mountaineering tourism and aims to provide policy suggestions for sustainable management of fragile mountain regions.

This will be of great interest to upper-level students and academics of tourism, as well as industry representatives and policymakers with an interest in adventure tourism and mountaineering.

Michal Apollo is an assistant professor at the Pedagogical University of Krakow, Institute of Geography, Department of Tourism and Regional Studies, a Fellow of Yale University's Global Justice Program, New Haven, USA, a Visiting Scholar at Hainan University-Arizona State University Joint International Tourism College, Haikou, China, and a Visiting Fellow at the Center for Tourism Research, Wakayama University, Japan.

Yana Wengel is an associate professor at Hainan University-Arizona State University Joint International Tourism College, Haikou, China and a Visiting Fellow at the Center for Tourism Research, Wakayama University, Japan.

Routledge Focus on Tourism and Hospitality

Routledge Focus on Tourism and Hospitality presents small books on big topics and how they intersect with the world of tourism and hospitality research. The idea is to fill the gap between journal article and book. This new short form series offers both established and early-career academics the flexibility to publish cutting-edge commentary on key areas of tourism and hospitality, topical issues, policy-focused research, analytical or theoretical innovations, a summary of the key players, or short topics for specialized audiences in a succinct way.

World Heritage and Tourism
Marketing and Management
Bailey Ashton Adie

Tourism and Urban Regeneration
Processes Compressed in Time and Space
Alberto Amore

Tourism, Sanctions and Boycotts
Siamak Seyfi and C. Michael Hall

Mountaineering Tourism
A Critical Perspective
Michal Apollo and Yana Wengel

For more information about this series, please visit: https://www.routledge.com/tourism/series/FTH

Mountaineering Tourism

A Critical Perspective

Michal Apollo and Yana Wengel

Routledge
Taylor & Francis Group

LONDON AND NEW YORK

First published 2022
by Routledge
2 Park Square, Milton Park, Abingdon, Oxon OX14 4RN

and by Routledge
605 Third Avenue, New York, NY 10158

Routledge is an imprint of the Taylor & Francis Group, an informa business

British Library Cataloguing-in-Publication Data
A catalogue record for this book is available from the British Library

Library of Congress Cataloging-in-Publication Data
Names: Apollo, Michał, author. | Wengel, Yana, author.
Title: Mountaineering tourism : a critical perspective /
Michal Apollo and Yana Wengel.
Description: Abingdon, Oxon ; New York, NY : Routledge, 2022. |
Series: Routledge focus on tourism and hospitality | Includes
bibliographical references and index.
Identifiers: LCCN 2021030730 (print) | LCCN 2021030731 (ebook)
Subjects: LCSH: Tourism. | Mountaineering.
Classification: LCC G155.A1 A5956 2022 (print) |
LCC G155.A1 (ebook) | DDC 338.4/791—dc23
LC record available at https://lccn.loc.gov/2021030730
LC ebook record available at https://lccn.loc.gov/2021030731

ISBN: 978-0-367-55829-1 (hbk)
ISBN: 978-0-367-55832-1 (pbk)
ISBN: 978-1-003-09532-3 (ebk)

DOI: 10.4324/9781003095323

Typeset in Times New Roman
by codeMantra

To our parents,
  Grażyna and Mieczysław [Michal's parents]
  Olga and Andrey [Yana's parents]
  Thank you for your unwavering support and
encouragement.

Contents

Figures

Tables

Foreword

Professor Dimitrios Buhalis
https://orcid.org/0000-0001-9148-6090

Mountain areas have always been a source of mysticism and inspiration for our society and culture. People have always gone to the mountains for agricultural reasons and also to reconnect with nature, adventure, and sport and for exploration, military conquest, and education. Traditionally, mountaineering was the preserve of experienced elite athletes who had the skills, self-sufficiency, and freedom needed to travel in the mountains. In the past, mountaineers gained gradual experience starting from smaller peaks before tackling the technically challenging high-altitude mountains. More recently, increased social engagement in mountaineering has changed the typical scene in mountaineering, promoting it as a recreation and tourism activity.

Recreation opportunities, and changes to the essential elements of what it means to be a mountaineer, have led to the commodification of the experience. Over the past two decades, the technology and the invention of new types of climbing equipment have expanded human capabilities allowing scientists, mountaineers, and travellers to popularise mountaineering. Travel to mountainous areas has quickly attracted the global tourist volume, making mountains the second most popular tourist attraction after coastal destinations. Investment, operation, and management decisions made by tour operators, other tourism professionals, and the entire industry help determine the extent of negative and positive impacts of mountain tourism. Therefore, it is crucial to cooperate with the sector to develop and promote sustainable tourism practices.

The undoubted merit of the book is the attempt to summarise various overlapping definitions relevant to the field and its laying the foundation of several terms, including mountaineering itself. Mountaineering activity is associated with overcoming numerous dangers associated with the terrain and meteorological conditions, and directly with the behaviours and actions of mountaineers. Hence, to succeed, mountaineers have to have excellent technical mountaineering skills and have interdisciplinary knowledge in a mountainous environment, human anatomy, and general physiology and behaviour. The book also draws attention to gaps in the mountaineering literature, including the true accessibility of mountaineering, human waste, and the balance of the high-mountain environment and altitude as the new host–guest reciprocity. Mountaineering interferes with and changes the environment in many different ways. With the influence of tourism (foreign cultures and ideas), economics, politics, social, cultural, and psychological conditions are also changing. Yet, with a planned and systematic approach, mountaineering can be a key factor in promoting an overall improvement in local people's quality of life through initiatives in economic development and environmental conservation.

This book by Michal Apollo and Yana Wengel, both experts in mountain science and tourism, and experienced mountaineers, with climbing successes all around the world, integrates knowledge from various perspectives into this under-researched area. The book includes both extensive research and the authors' personal mountaineering experience. Thus, this book is written by academics and professional mountaineers, who also made achievements in alpinism. The authors have also developed the entry on 'mountaineering tourism', which is published in the *Encyclopedia of Tourism Management and Marketing* (Edward Elgar Publishing).

Based on previous research and own expedition experience, the authors characterise the difficulties and dangers of mountains, formulate and classify the basic rules that must be observed to ensure safety while travelling in mountainous areas, and talk about ethics in mountaineering.

The undoubted advantage of this book is that it is written by mountain lovers for mountain lovers. From a tourist to a mountain tourism researcher, everyone will find a full range of knowledge here and will be motivated to explore mountains nearby and afield.

Professor Dimitrios Buhalis
Bournemouth University, UK
May 2021

Preface

Mountaineering Tourism: A Critical Perspective provides essential knowledge about mountaineering tourism and gives an overview of recent developments linked to the diversification, commodification, and commercialisation of mountaineering activity. This is the first book to disentangle overlapping terms and definitions related to mountaineering tourism. Mountaineering, broadly defined as hiking, trekking, and climbing, is now a mass tourism phenomenon, with continually growing numbers of trekkers, climbers, and religious tourists who hike in mountain regions.

The environments around high-mountain areas and their local resident communities, until recently cut off from civilisation, are sensitive to outside influences and have been abruptly exposed to the impact of mountaineering and related activities. The natural and built environments of mountain regions have been affected by an increasing number of visitors in recent decades, and, hence, the current policies concerning mountaineering tourism require updating, as proposed in this book.

Mountaineering Tourism: A Critical Perspective is a comprehensive summary of the development of mountaineering and its relationship with tourism. It is aimed at students, academics, industry representatives, and policymakers with an interest in adventure tourism and mountaineering.

Michal Apollo and Yana Wengel

1 Introduction to mountaineering

Abstract

Mountains of different heights and a wide range of shapes, climates, and ecosystems cover 25 per cent of the earth's surface. They have fascinated humans for thousands of years. This chapter looks at the early relationships between humans and mountains and provides a historical snapshot of the evolution of mountaineering and its connection to tourism. It also frames the term 'mountaineering tourism' from an ontological perspective and discusses the increasing popularity of mountaineering.

1.1 Mountains and humans

The definitions of mountainous areas are unavoidably arbitrary (Messerli & Ives, 1997). Usually, no qualitative or even quantitative distinction is made between mountains and hills (Barry, 2008). In simple terms, a mountain is a landform that rises prominently above its surroundings, generally exhibiting steep slopes, a relatively confined summit area, and considerable local relief. The mechanisms of the formation of mountains result from plate tectonics and, more precisely, are a consequence of their collisions. Ollier (1981) distinguishes four types of collision: (1) continent–continent collision (Himalayan type); (2) continent–ocean collision, related to the continent's overhang and subduction of the ocean floor (Andean type); (3) the collision of the continent with the ocean floor and the associated advance of oceanic sediments under the continent, followed by the uplift of the edge of the continent; and (4) thickening of the earth's crust as a result of a plate collision, possibly with the accompanying gravity flow of rocks close to the surface. Mountain ranges resulting from continent–continent

DOI: 10.4324/9781003095323-1

and continent–ocean collisions are most likely the dominant geological formation on the earth's surface (Dewey & Burke, 1973). For the purpose of this book, we will use a simple genetic system of mountain types, which was developed before global plate tectonics (mentioned above) was understood but is nevertheless valuable for local-scale understanding. There are five main types of mountains: volcanic, fold, plateau, fault-block, and dome (Goudie, 2004).

Humboldt (1849) and Darwin (1882) state that an environment's sensitivity increases with altitude gain. Today, altitudinal zonation represents a core concept in research on mountain environments (Apollo & Andreychouk, 2022; Apollo et al., 2020). Overall, a higher elevation produces colder climates than at sea level by deforming climatic zones, creating an aspherical Koppen's climate H (in German: Hochgebirge; in English: High mountains; Beniston, 2006; Ekhart, 1948). These colder climates have a significant effect on the ecosystems of mountains: different elevations have different plants and animals. Moreover, some species found in altitudinal zones become isolated since the conditions above and below a particular zone are inhospitable and constrain movements or dispersal (Barry, 2008). Mountains are usually characterised as inaccessible, fragile, diversified, and marginal areas (Messerli & Ives, 1997); therefore, over the ages, most mountain ecosystems remained in isolation from the outside world, as reflected in marginalised or lower-income communities.

Since time immemorial, humans have penetrated further and higher into mountains for hunting, and, later, seeking areas convenient for agriculture (Zurick & Pacheco, 2006). They learned to use local raw materials (mainly wood), build houses, and prepare farmland and pastures. Clear examples of such activities are abundant in high-mountain regions (Barry, 2008). Excessive exploitation of limited resources and ill-considered human activities (see, for example, Apollo, 2017a) combined with the highly dynamic population growth lead to degradation of the mountain environment and ecosystem services such as headwater catchment areas.

Since ancient times, humans have been fascinated by mountains. The Greeks worshipped Mount Olympus and considered it the territory of the gods, and in Asia as well mountains such as Mount Fuji in Japan and the many Himalayan peaks are considered holy and sacrosanct by the local population (Langdon, 2000; Macfarlane, 2009). As such, the names of many mountains by and large have a celestial origin; for example, 'Holy Mother' is the Tibetan name for Mount Chomolungma and the Tanzanian indigenous population living in regions around Mount Kilimanjaro call it the 'Abode of Cold God' (Salkeld,

2002; Thomson, 2012). Ancient people and pagan tribes have been worshipping the mountains since ages, as they believe that mountains possess mysterious, divine, and supernatural powers. For example, in New Zealand, Mount Taranaki has profound spiritual significance for Māori people and is seen as a life force (Langdon, 2000; Smith, 1997). Ancient beliefs depicting high mountains as the abode of gods, monsters, and dragons meant that early trips into the mountains were dangerous. Initially, this challenge was perversely undertaken by knowledge-seeking explorers, bold adventurers, and determined settlers. With the development of trade, people (especially merchants) were forced to search for transit routes through mountain ranges. However, getting to know the high mountains has always been the work of the first explorers – mountaineering pioneers. That is why the history of the conquest of mountains is best described through the history of mountaineering, the development and transformation of which influenced the overall activity of humans in high mountains over the years.

There are historical accounts that humans climbed mountains hundreds of years ago. For example, human footprints from the 2nd to 1st century BC were found at an altitude of almost 3,000 m at Mount Riffelhorn (Switzerland; Engel, 1950). Among the first-known ascents were the ascent to Mount Haemus (or Haemus Mons) in Thrace (a peak in the Balkan Mountain Range in Bulgaria) in 181 BC by the Macedonian King Philip V; Alexander the Great's climb up one of the peaks of the Siachen mountain range (Asia Minor) in 334 BC; and King Hadrian's journey to the top of the Etna volcano in AD 126 (Mayor, 2021). During the Inca Empire, humans built altars at Mount Llullaillaco at an elevation of 6,715 m (Ceruti, 2015), and Native Americans travelled extensively through the mountain passes (Rockwell, 2002). These prehistoric mountaineering accounts testify that people have had an interest in climbing mountain peaks since ancient times.

1.2 Mountaineering tourism: the term

Historically, the term 'mountaineering' (also 'mountain climbing' or 'alpinism') referred to the set of actions that led to the ascent of a mountain peak. At the beginning of the 20th century, mountaineering (in German: Bergsteigen; in Spanish: montañismo) was treated as an 'elite activity'. Before its commercialisation in the late 20th century, mountaineering referred to an unmediated encounter between a human and a mountain, without any artificial aids or the benefit of a guide (Holt, 2008).

The meaning of the term 'mountaineering' has been redefined and reinvented over several decades, and mountaineering activities have been subdivided into several categories. However, the terms overlap and a wide range of tourism activities in mountain environments are labelled as 'mountaineering' (Apollo, 2017b; Beedie & Hudson, 2003). Recently, the boundaries between mountaineering and tourism throughout the world have become increasingly blurred. Due to diversification, commodification, and commercialisation, mountaineering is becoming more of a mass tourism than an elite sports activity (Beedie & Hudson, 2003; Johnston & Edwards, 1994). While some scholars identify mountaineering-related activities as climbing (rock and ice) and trekking up mountains (Whitlock et al., 1991), others also add backpacking, hiking, skiing, via ferrata, and wilderness activities (Pomfret, 2006). Others again state that mountaineering activities also include indoor climbing, and climbing and bouldering sports (Coalter et al., 2010). Apollo (2021) subdivides mountaineering into three categories: (1) climbing (which now refers to adventure climbing or sports climbing), (2) trekking, and (3) hiking (hill walking in the mountains). As a part of the adventure tourism segment, mountaineering tourism is a subset of mountain tourism (a tourism activity in a mountain environment; Apollo & Wengel, 2021).

1.3 Development of mountaineering

Mountaineering evolved through several stages across the history of the development and evolution of human presence on mountains. Extending the previous work of Kiełkowska and Kiełkowski (2003), we identified the six stages of mountaineering: pre-alpinism, early mountaineering, classic mountaineering, modern mountaineering, contemporary mountaineering, and commercial mass mountaineering (Table 1.1).

Table 1.1 Stages of mountaineering development

1	Before 1786	Pre-mountaineering
2	1786–1864	Early mountaineering
3	1864–1899	Classic mountaineering
4	1900–1964	Modern mountaineering
5	1964–2021	Contemporary mountaineering
6	2021 onwards	Commercial mass mountaineering

Pre-mountaineering was the period of development evidenced by the early interaction between humans and mountains. It lasted from ancient times until Mont Blanc (4,810 m) was scaled in 1786. This period did not affect the development of high-mountain climbing as such but contributed to the recognition and accessibility of high-mountain regions. While searching for a route through mountains or for places for settlement, humans discovered 'white spots' on maps, and as people reached some peaks, mountaineering started to evolve from this climbing activity. In the past, a frequent motivation to approach a mountain or to reach its top was spiritual and based on faith. As such, the Greeks paid tribute to the gods who lived on Mount Olympus (2,918 m), the Maasai worshipped the gods of Mount Kilimanjaro (5,895 m), and some of the highest peaks of the Andes were visited for religious pilgrimage. To date, Judaists and Christians still visit the biblical mountain, Sinai, currently called Mount Jebel Musa (2,285 m). One of the earliest accounts of ascending a high mountain comes from the Holy Scriptures (2003, Ex. 19:20) – a record of Moses ascending Mount Sinai. The pre-mountaineering period became famous as the era of great geographical discoveries in high mountains.

The mid-18th century was the starting point of mountaineering in its modern sense and the beginning of the **early mountaineering** stage. In 1786, Jacques Balmat and Michel Paccard reached the summit of Mont Blanc (4,808 m), the highest peak in the Alps. The years between 1854 and 1865 were called the 'Golden Age of Mountaineering', a period during which most of the Alps' peaks were climbed. At this stage, the peaks were reached by the most accessible routes. Most of the peaks were conquered by British alpinists with the help of qualified guides from France and Switzerland. The Alps was the most popular location for climbing; however, small-scale expeditions were carried out outside of Europe, primarily by scientists. This period stands out as scientific pursuits were integrated into mountaineering, and many climbers carried with them instruments to conduct scientific observations at mountain peaks (Braham, 2004). This period also marked the establishment of the first mountaineering organisations, including the Alpine Club, the world's first mountaineering club, formed in 1857.

The period of **classic mountaineering** lasted from 1864 to the end of the 19th century. In 1865, English climbers scaled the Matterhorn (4,478 m) on a technically difficult path, which led to the popularisation of ascending a peak over a challenging path. The classic mountaineering period was characterised by the rapid development of high-mountain climbing. However, it was still centred in Europe. Gradually, guided mountaineering gave way to mountaineering without a guide. Slow-climbing exploration of the Caucasus Mountains, the Andes, Cordillera, and even the Southern Alps began. The mountains of Central Asia, including the Himalayas, were still poorly understood. During the classic period, mountaineering developed into its modern form, with a large body of professional guides, equipment, and methodologies (Hansen, 2013).

The period of **modern mountaineering** started from the beginning of the 20th century and carried on until 1964, when the last of 148,000-m peak was reached (excluding a subsidiary peak to Lhotse-Lhotse Middle 8,410 m). Overcoming extreme climbing routes in the European mountains, mountaineers further explored the Andes, Cordillera, and polar mountains and began high-altitude mountaineering on the peaks of Central Asia. In 1907, the era of high-altitude mountaineering was initiated by the first ascent over 7,000 m, when the summit of Mount Trisul I (7,120 m) was reached by a British expedition team led by Tom George Longstaff (Mason, 1955). In 1950, members of a French team, Maurice Herzog and Louis Lachenal, conquered the first 8,000-m peak, Annapurna I (8,091 m) (Herzog, 1952), and the highest peak in the world, Chomolungma or Everest (8,848 m), was reached by a British expedition led by John Hunt, New Zealander Edmund Hillary, and Sherpa Tenzing Norgay in 1953. Although the development of mountaineering was interrupted during the First and Second World Wars, the second half of the 20th century was the era of conquering the world's 8,000-m peaks.

The **contemporary mountaineering** period started once the last remaining 8,000-m peak was reached in 1964 and lasted until the last of the eight-thousanders was scaled in winter. Age-old climbing problems were dealt with by making crossings on the world's most enormous and difficult cliffs. Several significant events took place between the 1980s and 2000s: Reinhold Messner made the first oxygen-free solo ascent of Mount Everest in 1980; American multimillionaire Richard Bass was the first person in the world to conquer the highest peak on each of the seven continents (now known as the Seven Summits Challenge); and in 2001 the Russian team stood on top of the 8,410-m-tall Lhotse Middle (Koshelenko, 2002). The Lhotse Middle is a subsidiary peak to Lhotse, which, despite an altitude of 8,410 m, does not appear in the classic list of 14 eight-thousanders. This, and above all its location on an extremely steep and rugged ridge, meant that it was one of the last of only about 30 peaks of over 8,000 m to remain unclimbed until 2001. The popularisation of mountaineering in the press and media, the creation of peak-bagging challenges (Chu et al., 2018; Lew & Han, 2015) like the Seven Summits (Bass et al., 1986), and the establishment of commercial Everest expeditions in the 1990s led to the development of mass mountaineering.

In 2021, the winter ascent to K2 by a team of Nepalese mountaineers, the most recent and perhaps most technically challenging mountaineering success to date, brought the contemporary mountaineering period to a close. The new period, **commercial mass mountaineering**, is expected to develop on a massive scale. Perhaps lower but more technically challenging mountains, such as Myanmar's Hkakabo Razi peak (5,881 m), might become a focus for elite mountaineers, while ordinary tourists may look to the popular mountains, which provide opportunities for serviced commercial mass mountaineering expeditions (Wengel et al., 2021).

For two centuries, mountaineering was an elite sport, but its popularity has grown in recent years, and many mountainous regions have developed products for various categories of mountaineering tourists. The popularity of mountaineering can be explained by the increased interest in nature among urban dwellers, in mountainous areas in particular, as well as the improved accessibility to mountaineering resources (Apollo, 2017b). These resources include nature (mountains and their environments) and all involved stakeholders, such as the International Climbing and Mountaineering Federation (Union Internationale des Associations d'Alpinisme (UIAA)), national associations and clubs, as well as search and rescue organisations, expedition companies, equipment manufacturers, and the local communities living and working in the mountains.

1.4 Evolution of mountaineering equipment

The right mountaineering equipment plays a critical role in an expedition, no matter how high the peak or how long the expedition. Mountaineering activities range from daytrips to expeditions lasting several weeks. The terrain of high-altitude mountain environments is mixed (with the presence of rock, ice, and snow), so climbers need to be able to navigate through a wide variety of conditions. Hence, during an expedition, mountaineers use a wide range of personal and communal technical equipment. The equipment helps mountaineers reach the summit and aids a safe descent. Insufficient or faulty equipment can lead to unfortunate accidents. Equipment can make the difference between life and death in some cases.

Since the late 19th century, mountaineering equipment has drastically improved due to the implementation of modern technology in manufacturing processes and the innovative materials used in products (including tents, sleeping bags, backpacks, shoes, clothes, and other equipment). This section provides an overview of the critical mountaineering equipment and how it has changed since the emergence of mountaineering as a sport.

Early mountaineers adapted regular clothes and used many layers of wool and cotton to survive in the harsh environments of high mountains. In the early 20th century, mountaineers used windproof and waterproof canvas developed for ocean travel to provide protection and insulation. Many of the natural fibres (especially wool and cotton) used in the early stages of mountaineering have since been replaced by synthetic fibres such as nylon, a synthetic thermoplastic polymer patented by DuPont in 1935 (E.I. du Pont de Nemours & Company, 1988). Advances in technology and manufacturing resulted in the creation of blends of synthetic and natural fibres, combining the best of both. In the 1970s, the advent of waterproof coatings and breathable textile laminates improved mountaineering attire. The development and diversification of mountaineering activities further advanced the tourism industry, mountaineering clothes and tools, and allowed climbing techniques to evolve in more sophisticated and specialised ways. Figure 1.1 illustrates some of the key modern climbing equipment, including

A   Fixed anchors: 1 – quick-draw, 2 – spit, 3 – ring, 4 – jumar;
B   Removable anchors: 1 – camming device, camalot type; 2 – camming device, nut rock type;

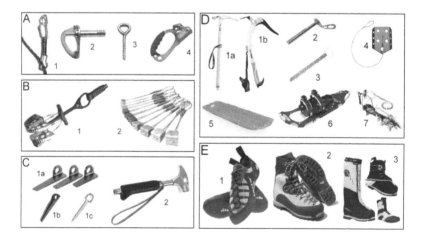

Figure 1.1 Modern climbing equipment.

C   Rock pitons: 1a – knife type, 1b – v type, 1c – diagonal type; 2 – piton hammer;
D   Winter climbing equipment: 1 – ice axe (1a – classic piolet, 1b – technical ice tool); 2 – ice screw; 3 – snow pickets; 4 – deadman, 5 – sleds; 6 – snowshoe; 7 – crampons;
E   Climbing shoes: 1 – rock-climbing type, 2 – alpine type, 3 – overboot type.

Currently, mountaineering equipment represents a high-tech multi-billion-dollar industry that provides more comfortable, lightweight, and durable clothing and equipment, hence offering more protection for mountaineers. Modern clothing and shoes benefit from high-tech materials such as Gore-Tex and Nikwax, which make fabrics waterproof and breathable at the same time. Tents have evolved from bulky and heavy canvas options to lighter compact versions, dominated by dome and wedge tents with tent poles made from aluminium, carbon fibre, or fibreglass. Modern sleeping bags can withstand freezing temperatures but remain lightweight. They are insulated with goose down or synthetic fibres. The evolution of some of the essential mountaineering equipment is described below.

Ropes: In the early stages of mountaineering, the role of rope in climbing was much more modest than it is today. In the 19th century, rope was just a 'guiding' tool connecting a team of climbers. It was possible to hold on to the rope during the ascent, but it could not withstand a climber's fall – an animal or plant fibre rope was not designed for this. During the first attempt to scale Mount Everest in the 1920s, Mallory and Irvine used linen ropes as they were slightly stronger and more elastic than hemp ropes. The invention of nylon revolutionised rope production technology. The first nylon ropes were produced in 1938, and the Second World War accelerated their spread and expanded possible applications. Nylon ropes have been used in climbing since the 1940s (Microys, 1977); they are strong, lightweight, and able to withstand a climber's weight in the case of a fall (Borwick, 1973).

The Kernmantle technology revolutionised climbing ropes when a strong synthetic nylon core was braided with external fibres, forming a kind of sheath. The extraordinary strength of these ropes has led to numerous changes in trends and directions in mountaineering. For example, climbing as a sport developed entirely due to the excellent dynamic properties of modern ropes. Modern rope technology, including the dynamic rope core twisting technique (increased elasticity and strength), solved two main problems: rope twisting and wear (Bright, 2014).

Harnesses: Perhaps the most controversial topic in the evolution of mountaineering gear was the method of belaying the climber. On many occasions, belay innovation was met with both enthusiasm and scepticism in the climbing community as some considered belay innovations unethical and contradictory to the 'spirit of real mountaineering'. One of the key pieces of belay equipment is a climbing harness. The invention of the climbing harness dates back to the late 19th century and was attributed to Jeanne Immink, a female Dutch climber (Muré, 2010). A sit-in type of climbing harness consists of a waist belt and leg loops; it was invented in 1960 by the Yosemite climbers. The harness is a piece of belay equipment that secures a climber to a rope or an anchor point (Eng, 2010).

Carabiners: The German climber and inventor Otto Herzog invented the first carabiner in 1910. Over the next 30 years, carabiners evolved from heavy, steel, pear-shaped devices to oval-shaped and then to light alloy carabiners, which have been used commercially since 1947. Modern carabiners exist in a pear shape, D shape, or asymmetric D shape. Gate-type carabiners include straight, bent, and wire gate, and there are four types of locks: snap gate, wire gate, screw gate, and twist gate (Bright, 2014).

Mechanical aids: Mountaineers use various types of mechanical aids for anchoring, attaching slings, and assisting the ascent and decent processes. All of these tools, including pitons, hooks, bolts, and chocks of various types and shapes, have improved through the history of mountaineering in terms of material and technology. The first pitons appeared in Europe at the end of the 19th century, and they were designed as simple hooks (without a ring or eye; the rope was tight around them) to fit cracks in rock. With the evolution of technology and metal manufacturing, Hans Fiechtl invented and produced modern pitons made of mild steel with an eye rather than an attached ring. By 1946, ultra-strong pitons for use on granite mountains were created.

Pitons were undoubtedly the very first mechanical aid that helped to create intermediate belay points on rocks and on mountains. In the 1970s, new tools that could be inserted into rock cracks were invented. Spring-loaded camming devices (also SLCD, cam, or friend) are protection devices designed to be placed in parallel-sided cracks to prevent the falling climber from hitting the ground. Another revolutionary mountaineering tool, hexentrics, large metal hexagonal-shaped wedges placed in rock cracks to provide protection or support for a climber, were developed by Yvon Chouinard, one of the leading climbers and equipment inventors in 1976 (Chouinard & Frost, 1976).

Furthermore, Chouinard and his partner, Frost, improved and reinvented other mountaineering tools, including crampons, ice axes, and ice screws. Other popular auxiliary aids include jumars, Salewa Hiebler ascenders, and Gibbs ascenders and are mainly used for vertical rope climbing (Eng, 2010).

Crampons and ice axes: Crampons are metal spikes that are attached to boots to ensure better traction and grip on hard snow and ice. In the late 19th century, crampons had four points, but they had evolved to have 12 points by 1932. Modern crampons are made of steel alloy, lightweight aluminium, or a combination of both metals. Another integral piece of mountaineering equipment is an ice axe. The ice axe is used to assist movement on ice, snow, and talus slopes as well as to enable support and self-belay on these types of terrain.

Ice axes have evolved from the alpenstock, which was popular from the end of the 19th to the middle of the 20th century. The alpenstock had a wooden shaft, a sharp steel tip (called a bayonet), and a spike; it was about 150 cm in length (Figure 1.2a). The Eisbeil (meaning 'ice tool' in German) was shorter than an alpenstock; its shaft was wooden, and it often had a hammer instead of a blade (adze) on its head and hence was used to install (hammer in) the pitons (Figure 1.2b).

Modern ice axes meet the design and manufacturing standards outlined by the Union Internationale des Associations d'Alpinisme (UIAA). There are two types of ice axe: basic (B/type 1) and technical (T/type 2). The basic ice axe (also called a mountaineering ice axe)

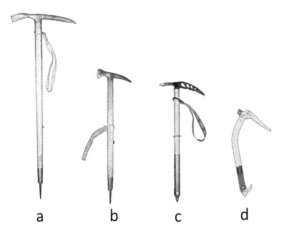

a   b   c   d

Figure 1.2 Types of ice axes (a – alpenstock, b – Eisbeil, c – basic ice axe [B/type 1], and d –technical ice axe [T/type 2]).

is used in snow conditions for essential support and self-arrest on a mountain (Figure 1.2c). The usual length of an ice axe, spike to head, ranges from 60 to 90 cm. Technical ice axes (also called ice tools) are shorter (40 to 60 cm in length) and have a curved shaft and a wide range of picks and adzes (Figure 1.2d). Ice tools are used two to a person for vertical or steep ice climbing and provide additional belaying in such conditions (Eng, 2010).

In terms of safety and certification, the UIAA began with rope testing in the 1960s. In the early 1970s, it created a safety commission that aimed to create standards for mountaineering equipment. Since then, the standards for over 20 types of safety equipment, including helmets, harnesses, and crampons, were developed. Since the 1990s, the UIAA has collaborated with the European Committee for Standardization, the American Society for Testing and Materials, and other organisations for the harmonisation of standards (www.theuiaa.org/safety/safety-standards).

References

Apollo, M. (2017a). The population of Himalayan regions – By the numbers: Past, present and future. In R. Efe & M. Öztürk (Eds.), *Contemporary studies in environment and tourism* (pp. 145–159). Cambridge Scholars Publishing.

Apollo, M. (2017b). The true accessibility of mountaineering: The case of the High Himalaya. *Journal of Outdoor Recreation and Tourism, 17*, 29–43. https://doi.org/10.1016/j.jort.2016.12.001

Apollo, M. (2021). *Environmental impacts of mountaineering: A conceptual framework*. Springer. https://doi.org/10.1007/978-3-030-72667-6

Apollo, M., & Andreychouk, V. (2022). Mountaineering adventure tourism and local communities: Social, environmental and economic interactions. Cheltenham: Edward Elgar Publishing.

Apollo, M., Andreychouk, V., Moolio, P., Wengel, Y., & Myga-Piątek, U. (2020). Does the altitude of habitat influence residents' attitudes to guests? A new dimension in the residents' attitudes to tourism. *Journal of Outdoor Recreation and Tourism*, 100312. https://doi.org/10.1016/j.jort.2020.100312

Apollo, M., & Wengel, Y. (2021). Mountaineering tourism. In D. Buhalis (Ed.), *Encyclopaedia of tourism management and marketing*. Edward Elgar Publishing Limited.

Barry, R. (2008). *Mountain weather and climate* (3rd ed.). Cambridge University Press.

Bass, R., Wells, F., & Ridgeway, R. (1986). *Seven summits*. Warner Books.

Beedie, P., & Hudson, S. (2003). Emergence of mountain-based adventure tourism. *Annals of Tourism Research, 30*(3), 625–643. https://doi.org/10.1016/S0160-7383(03)00043-4

Beniston, M. (2006). Mountain weather and climate: A general overview and a focus on climatic change in the Alps. *Hydrobiologia, 562*, 3–16.

Borwick, G. R. (1973). Mountaineering ropes. *The Alpine Journal, 1*, 67–70.

Braham, T. (2004). *When the Alps cast their spell: Mountaineers of the Alpine Golden Age.* In Pinn.

Bright, C. M. (2014). *A history of rock climbing gear technology and standards* [Honors Thesis, University of Arkansas]. Fayetteville. http://scholarworks. uark.edu/meeguht/41

Ceruti, M. C. (2015). Frozen Mummies from Andean Mountaintop Shrines: Bioarchaeology and Ethnohistory of Inca Human Sacrifice. *BioMed Research International, 2015*, 439428. https://doi.org/10.1155/2015/439428

Chouinard, Y., & Frost, T. (1976). *Irregular, polygonal mountaineering chock.* United States Patent No. U. S. P. Office.

Chu, Q., Grühn, D., & Holland, A. M. (2018). Life is short – Make a bucket list: How age and time horizon impact motivations. *Innovation in Aging, 2*(1), 754. https://doi.org/10.1093/geroni/igy023.2786

Coalter F, Dimeo P, Morrow S & Taylor J (2010). *The Benefits of Mountaineering and Mountaineering Related Activities: A Review of Literature: A Report to the Mountaineering Council of Scotland.* Mountaineering Council of Scotland; British Mountaineering Council. Department of Sports Studies, University of Stirling.

Darwin, C. (1882). *The origin of species by means of natural selection: Or the preservation of favored races in the struggle for life.* D. Appleton and Company.

Dewey, J. F., & Burke, K. (1973). Tibetan, Variscan and Precambrian basement reactivation: Products of continental collision. *The Journal of Geology, 81*, 683–692.

E.I. du Pont de Nemours & Company. (1988). *Nylon: A DuPont Invention.* https://digital.hagley.org/islandora/search/mods_relatedItem_host_titleInfo_title_ms%3A%22Pam%5C%2099.008%22

Ekhart, E. (1948). De la structure de l'atmosphe're dans la montagne. *La Me'te'orologie* (3), 3–26.

Eng, R. C. (2010). *Mountaineering: The Freedom of the Hills.* Mountaineers Books.

Engel, C. E. (1950). *A history of mountaineering in the Alps.* George Allen & Unwin.

Goudie, A. S. (2004). *Encyclopedia of geomorphology.* Routledge.

Hansen, P. H. (2013). *The summits of modern man.* Harvard University Press.

Herzog, M. (1952). *Annapurna: First conquest of an 8000-meter peak.* E. P. Dutton & Co.

Holt, L. W. (2008). *Mountains, mountaineering and modernity: A cultural history of German and Austrian mountaineering, 1900–1945.* [The University of Texas]. Austin. http://hdl.handle.net/2152/3901

Humboldt, A. v. (1849). *Aspects of nature, in different lands and different climates with scientific elucidations* (3rd ed.). J. Murray. https://www. biodiversitylibrary.org/item/99042

Johnston, B. R., & Edwards, T. (1994). The commodification of mountaineering. *Annals of Tourism Research, 21*(3), 459–478. https://doi.org/10.1016/0160-7383(94)90114-7

Kiełkowska, M., & Kiełkowski, J. (Eds.). (2003). *Wielka encyklopedia gór i alpinizmu*. Wydawnictwo Stapis.

Koshelenko, Y. (2002). Unraveling the mystery of Lhotse Middle. *American Alpine Journal, 44*(76). http://publications.americanalpineclub.org/articles/12200216600/Unraveling-the-Mystery-of-Lhotse-Middle

Langdon, M. K. (2000). Mountains in Greek religion. *The Classical World, 93*(5), 461–470. https://doi.org/10.2307/4352439

Lew, A. A., & Han, G. (2015). A world geography of mountain trekking. In G. Musa, J. Higham, & A. Thompson-Carr (Eds.), *Mountaineering tourism* (pp. 19–39). Routledge.

Macfarlane, R. (2009). *Mountains of the mind: Adventures in reaching the summit*. Knopf Doubleday Publishing Group.

Mason, K. (1955). *Abode of snow: A history of Himalayan exploration and mountaineering*. Rupert Hart-Davis.

Mayor, A. (2021). *Who were the first recreational mountain climbers?* Retrieved 27/03/2021 from https://www.wondersandmarvels.com/2013/06/who-were-the-first-recreational-mountain-climbers.html

Messerli, B., & Ives, J. (1997). *Mountains of the world: A global priority*. Parthenon Publishing.

Microys, H. F. (1977). Climbing ropes. *American Alpine Journal*. http://publications.americanalpineclub.org/articles/12197713000/Climbing-Ropes

Muré, H. (2010). *Jeanne Immink. Die Frau, die in die Wolken stieg*. Tyrolia.

Ollier, C.D. (1981). *Tectonics and landforms*. Longman.

Pomfret, G. (2006). Mountaineering adventure tourists: A conceptual framework for research. *Tourism Management, 27*(1), 113–123. https://doi.org/10.1016/j.tourman.2004.08.003

Rockwell, D. (2002). *Exploring Glacier National Park*. Globe Pequot Press.

Salkeld, A. (2002). *Kilimanjaro: To the roof of Africa*. National Geographic Society.

Smith, A. (1997). Who is that mountain standing there … its Taranaki. In B. Messerli & J. Ives (Eds.), *In mountains of the world: A global priority*. Parthenon Publishing.

Thomson, T. (2012). *Western Himalaya and Tibet: A narrative of a journey through the mountains of Northern India, during the years 1847–8*. Cambridge University Press.

Wengel, Y., Aye, N., Pyar, W. Y. K., & Kreisz, J. (2021). Mountainous protected areas in Myanmar: Current conditions and the outlook for nature-based tourism. In Jones, T.m Bui, H., & Apollo, M. (Eds.), *Nature-based tourism in Asia's mountainous protected areas* (pp. 197–220). Springer.

Whitlock, W., Van Romer, K., & Becker, H. (Eds.). (1991). *Nature based tourism: An Annotated bibliography*. Strom Thurmond Institute, Regional Development Group.

Zurick, D. N., & Pacheco, J. (2006). *Illustrated Atlas of the Himalaya*. The University Press of Kentucky.

2 Mountaineering as a form of tourism

Abstract

This chapter reviews and defines the types and divisions of mountaineering. It describes grades of mountaineering in each category (hiking, trekking, and mountain climbing). Furthermore, it illustrates the development of the accessibility of mountaineering and examines the grades in more depth. Finally, it considers the core medical issues related to the human body's adaptation to a high-altitude environment and what can cause negative consequences and issues when there are no proper acclimatisation procedures in place.

2.1 Mountaineering: divisions and types

Mountaineering refers to human climbing activity in high mountains, ranging from high-mountain hiking to mountaineering. Mountaineering has, in a similar way to other forms of qualified tourism, undergone far-reaching specialisation over the years. In this way, it covers a wide range of activities – from short routes in relatively easy terrain several hours away from civilisation to demanding and multiday climbing in remote and inaccessible mountains. In both cases, regardless of the technical difficulty or duration, a hiker or climber is exposed to a number of dangers associated with the high-mountain environment. Eng (2014) divides these dangers into two categories: (a) objective dangers arising from the characteristics of the terrain and mountain climate and over which the tourist has no influence, and (b) subjective dangers resulting from various weaknesses of the human body, insufficient physical and technical preparation, lack of appropriate equipment, and mistakes made.

DOI: 10.4324/9781003095323-2

Apollo (2021) subdivides mountaineering activity into three main categories:

- Hiking – an activity that exposes participants to objective and subjective dangers. Hiking takes place on well-prepared routes (both logistically and in terms of infrastructure). Individuals engaged in hiking move in the terrain without the use of their hands to overcome obstacles.
- Trekking – a more challenging activity that also exposes participants to danger (objective and subjective). While trekking, individuals may occasionally use their hands to overcome some obstacles. Trekking usually takes place in alpine terrain devoid of tourist infrastructure. Alpine trekking is an intermediate form between hiking and climbing that has evolved from hiking. Currently, hiking in mountainous areas is considered trekking; however, the word's initial meaning referred to hiking in the wild, dangerous Himalayas. These days, the development of tourism infrastructure in many regions has deprived trekking of its original 'wild' and 'off-the-beaten-track' setting. Furthermore, 'trekking' is often incorrectly used synonymously with 'hiking tourism', regardless of where and how it occurs.
- Climbing – the most dangerous form of mountaineering activity, taking place on high mountains above the forest line. Climbing exposes participants to danger (objective and subjective), and the demanding terrain requires the active use of legs and hands to overcome obstacles. Mountain climbing is often identified as alpinism, from climbing activity in the Alps; however, every alpine climbing activity, even in the Himalayas or Andes, is considered alpinism as well.

Figure 2.1 represents the zones for each mountaineering activity. All mountaineering forms can also be divided into two other categories: organised mountaineering (usually organised by trekking companies that employ mountaineering guides) and unorganised activity (Apollo, 2017; Kiełkowska & Kiełkowski, 2003).

Both ascending high-mountain peaks (alpine climbing) and traversing alpine terrain (alpine hiking) in remote regions of the world require much dedication, effort, and time. Therefore, tourism in high mountains often requires serious organisational commitment or even takes the form of an expedition. During organised mountaineering activity, tourists employ a guiding company that organises all logistics (e.g. visas, entry permits, route planning, and activities during the trek). Furthermore, trekking tourists and mountaineers often need to trek to the location from which they can start climbing – a base camp, for example. As a rule, they are accompanied by professional guides and porters

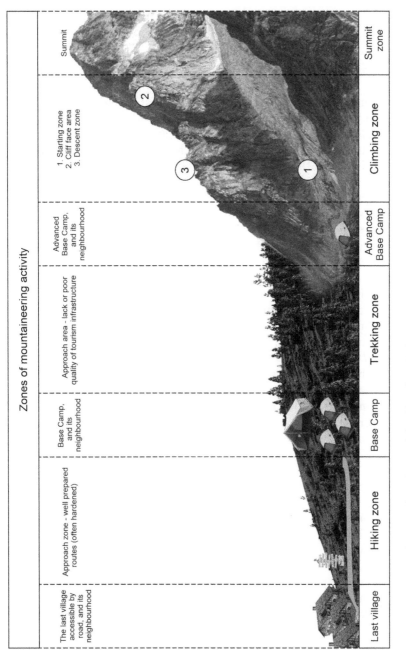

Figure 2.1 Zones of mountaineering activity (Apollo, 2021).

(individuals employed to carry tourists' belongings and expedition supplies).

Furthermore, mountaineering activity can also be categorised by (1) climbing season, (2) climbing techniques, and (3) type of ground (e.g. see Apollo, 2014; Eng, 2010; Hattingh, 2000; Kiełkowska & Kiełkowski, 2003).

1   Climbing season: mountaineering can be split into two seasonal categories, which are determined by the weather conditions:
   • *Summer mountaineering* – summit ascents or path crossings in the primary climbing season characterised by the best (optimal) weather and snow conditions for alpine activity, when statistically the summit is reached by the most people. Often this period does not coincide with the calendar summer. For example, in the Himalayas, it falls in spring and autumn.
   • *Winter mountaineering* – a more challenging and demanding activity as the conditions are less favourable, and access to base camps and summits is not easy. Furthermore, winter mountaineering is arduous and has as much to do with the mental challenge as it does with physical endurance and the successful application of technical skills.
2   Climbing technique: mountaineering can be subdivided into two forms depending on the use of auxiliary tools:
   • *Traditional climbing* – moving (climbing) only with the use of the natural relief. Climbing equipment is for belaying only. Many climbers refer to the classic form only for rock climbing activity, thus excluding any winter activity and considering crampons and ice axes – necessary in ice – as elements of facilitation, which in a way constitutes the arming of arms and legs (Eng, 2010; Hattingh, 2000; Kiełkowska & Kiełkowski, 2003).
   • *Climbing with supplementary tools* – moving (climbing) in the terrain using artificial facilities for moving (Eng, 2014; Hattingh, 2000; Kiełkowska & Kiełkowski, 2003). In the highest mountains, apart from artificial steps and grips (e.g. hooks, ankles), there may be ladders, hanging bridges, and rails; furthermore, many mountaineers also rely on supplemental oxygen cylinders (Kiełkowska & Kiełkowski, 2003).
3   Type of ground: mountaineering can also be classified according to the type of substrate:
   • *Rock climbing* – moving (climbing) in rocky terrain not covered with ice or snow.
   • *Ice climbing* – moving (climbing) in an area covered with ice and fern – steep snow corners, icefalls (frozen waterfalls), and various icicle formations, for example.

- *Snow climbing* – moving (climbing) in glacier mountains and engaging in mountaineering during the winter.
- *Mixed climbing* – a climbing style that requires the use of both rock and ice techniques (Eng, 2010; Hattingh, 2000; Kiełkowska & Kiełkowski, 2003).

2.2 Grades of mountaineering (subdivided into hiking, trekking, and mountain climbing)

Depending on the requirements and technical difficulties, hiking and climbing routes are defined using graded levels of difficulty. The scales help participants to choose a path that will not only be a challenge but also one within the limits of their abilities. The scales of difficulty exist in various disciplines of mountain activity. In the diverse forms of mountain-based tourism, there are scales for, among others, tourist routes, via ferratas, rock climbing (classic), bouldering, ice, snow or mixed climbing, hook climbing, rafting on mountain rivers, and downhill skiing. Each of the above disciplines has different classification types for the scale: adjective (strong or weak difficulty), digital (Arabic or Roman), letter (lowercase, uppercase), or mixed numbers and letters (alphanumeric). They may have a plus or minus sign indicating the upper or lower limit of the step. In addition, there are often several scales, even in one discipline. For example, difficulties in rock climbing are determined by, for example, the French scale or the Union Internationale des Associations d'Alpinisme (UIAA) scale (Eng, 2010; Jodłowski, 2011; Kiełkowska & Kiełkowski, 2003).

The scales of difficulty start with an easy (straight) hike, for which the first, lowest step is usually reserved, and end with an extreme climb. This approach is reflected in the UIAA scale, in which it is Grade I that determines tourist routes. In his Tatra Scale, Paryski (1951, 1976) divided the first degree of the UIAA scale into four grades: 0− (no difficulty), 0 (very easy), 0+ (easy), and I (a little difficult; hands are sometimes used to maintain balance). The remaining routes (above UIAA Grade I) require proper climbing preparation and specialist equipment (Radwańska-Paryska & Paryski, 1995). However, even then, a number of facilities (railings, ladders, etc.) on routes above UIAA Grade I make them often available to tourists, though only those at an advanced level. The best example of this type of route is the iron pier. Removing a number of facilitations would result in transition to a much higher difficulty level, possibly the second degree of the UIAA scale (Kiełkowska & Kiełkowski, 2003). Table 2.1 provides a summary and comparison of the scales of difficulty used for rock climbing in different countries (Haciski, 2013).

In the 1920s, Welzenbach created a 6-point scale, used later (1937) to introduce the USA's Sierra Club System scale. After minor modifications, it became a scale commonly used all over the world, known as the Yosemite or YDS (Yosemite Decimal System) scale (Eng, 2010; Isserman, 2016). YDS works best in describing the difficulties of high-altitude-climbing tourism, dividing it into five classes denoted by Arabic numerals, with the fifth class having a fractional extension. The YDS scale is divided into classes based on the technical and physical difficulties encountered:

- Class 1 – hiking.
- Class 2 – easy steep terrain. Hands are required sometimes.
- Grade 3 – very easy climbing. Rope is needed sometimes.
- Grade 4 – easy climbing. Often in exposed terrain (land relief). Rope is often used. Falling without belaying while climbing will result in death. The route is equipped with natural belaying points.
- Grade 5 – serious rock climbing. It is necessary to use a rope, belaying posts (from which the climber is secured at a particular moment), and artificial belaying points. It is possible to have a long, 'in flight' fall. The actual difficulties of the route are indicated by the number after the dot.

However, each valuation is subjective and influenced by a number of factors. For example, the given difficulty always assumes that the weather conditions are favourable and that the climber has the right equipment. The sense of difficulty is also influenced by other variables, such as the height, strength, and flexibility[1] of the climber, as well as the nature of the climb (Eng, 2010). The determination of the degree of difficulty of a given route does not yet constitute its full assessment; the latter purpose is served by additional data in the description of the route and in its sketch or diagram: the accumulation of difficulties, exposure, rock brittleness, wall height, and so on (Radwańska-Paryska & Paryski, 1995). A comparison of the most well-known and commonly used valuations of rock passes, although only illustrative due to the controversy related to their creation and juxtaposition, is presented in Table 2.1.

Contrary to the classification of routes in classic climbing, the evaluation and division of the difficulty of ice and snow routes is more complex in its nature. This is clearly hindered by the changing nature of the route, which is modified from season to season, and sometimes even during the day (due to melting). Above the line of eternal snow and on glaciers, the difficulties are defined based on the complications of climbing, the thickness of the ice, and the elements of its sculpture in the form of icicles, cauliflowers, and slings (Eng, 2010). On an 8-point scale, the following were distinguished (Kiełkowska & Kiełkowski, 2003):

Table 2.1 Comparison of the classification of the difficulty of rock-climbing routes in different countries

YDS (USA)	British (UK)		Francuska	UIAA	Ewbank (Australia)	GDR (West Europe)	Finnish	Brazilian	North Africa	Poland (Kurtyka's scale[a])
	Tech	Opis								
5.2		M	1	I				Isup	8	I
5.3		D	2	II	11			II	10	II
5.4			2+	II+	12			IIsup	11	II+
5.5		VD	3	III				III	12	III+
5.6	4a	S	4	IV	13		5−	IIIsup	13	IV
5.7	4b	HS	4+	V−	14		5	IV	14	IV+
			5		15				15	V−
5.8	4c	VS	5+	V	16	VIIa	5+	IVsup	16	V
5.9		HVS		V+	17	VIIb	6−	V	17	V+
5.10a		E1		VI−	18	VIIc		VI	18	V+/VI−
5.10b					19			VI/VI+	19	VI−
5.10c	5a		6a	VI	20	VIIIa	6	VIsup/VI+	20	VI
5.10d	5b	E2	6a+	VI+	21	VIIIb	6+	VIsup	21	VI+
5.11a			6b	VII−	22	VIIIc		7a	22	VI.1
5.11b			6b+	VII	23			7b	23	VI.1+
5.11c	5c	E3	6c	VII+	24	IXa	7−	7c	24	VI.2
5.11d			6c+	VIII−	25	IXb	7	8a	25	VI.2+
5.12a	6a	E4	7a	VIII	26	IXc	7+	8b	26	VI.2+/VI.3
5.12b	6b		7a+				8−	8c		VI.3
5.12c	6c	E5	7b	VIII+	27	Xa	8	9a	27	VI.3+
5.12d			7b+	IX−	28	Xb	8+	9b	28	VI.4

(Continued)

YDS (USA)	British (UK)		Francuska	UIAA	Ewbank (Australia)	GDR (West Europe)	Finnish	Brazilian	North Africa	Poland (Kurtyka's scale[a])
	Tech	Opis								
5.13a		E6	7c	IX	29	Xc	9−	9c	29	VI.4+
5.13b			7c+	IX+			9		30	VI.5
5.13c	7a		8a	X−	30		9+	10a	31	VI.5+
5.13d		E7	8a+	X	31		10−	10b	32	VI.5+/VI.6
5.14a	7b		8b	X+	32		10	10c	33	VI.6
5.14b	7c		8b+				10+	11a	34	VI.6+
5.14c		E8	8c	XI−	33		11−	11b	35	VI.7
5.14d	8a		8c+	XI	34		11	11c	36	VI.7+
5.15a			9a		35			12a	37	VI.8
			9a+							
			9b							
			9b+							

Source: Haciski (2013).
[a] From the inventor Wojciech Kurtyka.

- Grade 1 – frozen lake or stream (ice rink).
- Grade 2 – short sections of ice with an inclination of up to 80° with good places for anchoring the belay.
- Grade 3 – ice with good consistency and a slope of up to 80°, in which setting the belay requires practice, although there are places to rest.
- Grade 4 – all or virtually all of the lift is vertical and littered with ice formations requiring the climber to use long passes.
- Grade 5 – long and demanding stretches of ice of up to 50 m with a slope of 85–90°, where skill in using belaying is required, and there are few or no places to rest.
- Grade 6 – a full 50-m lift of vertical ice (e.g. often of poor quality – brittle), requiring the installation of the belay in uncomfortable positions.
- Grade 7 – a full 50-m lift of vertical or overhang ice of questionable quality, requiring physical and mental resistance, as well as high efficiency and creativity.
- Grade 8 – the (most difficult[2]) extreme ice climb requiring courage and gymnastic fitness.

Depending on the nature of the climb, the Arabic numeral showing the degree is usually preceded by letters: in the case of icefalls, WI (water ice) or M (mixed – mixed climbing: rock–ice routes). Difficulties with snow passes are usually defined by the angle of the slope of snow cover and range from 0° to 90°. The grading of a climbing route in high mountains is usually determined by indicating the values of all the elements it contains. In other words, for the assessment of a route containing rock, snow, ice, and mixed sections, all the scales described above are used. The American National Climbing Classification System's (NCCS) scale precedes the total valuation used to break down the difficulties in high mountains. On a 7-point scale, it describes the difficulties of high-mountain climbing, distinguishing:

- Grade I – climbing usually taking several hours and possibly having some technical difficulties.
- Grade II – half-day climbing, which may have some technical difficulties.
- Grade III – full-day climbing, which may have some technical difficulties.
- Grade IV – climbing takes the whole day; the most challenging part is no less than 5.7 on the YDS scale.
- Grade V – climbing takes one-and-a-half days; the most difficult section is more than 5.8 on the YDS scale.

- Grade VI – multiday climbing, very demanding classic or hook climbing.
- Grade VII – multiday climbing, very demanding classic or hook climbing in a region remote from civilisation, where a possible rescue operation is difficult or even impossible.

2.3 Accessibility and mountaineering

According to Middleton (1994), accessibility to typical destinations includes the components of infrastructure (roads, airports, railways, seaports), equipment (size, speed, and range of public transport vehicles), operational factors (routes operated, frequency of services, prices), and government regulations regarding transportation (Candela & Figini, 2012; Dwyer & Kim, 2003; Mayor, 2021; Prideaux, 2000). However, a profound understanding of the combination of physical, natural, social, and managerial conditions that grant value to a mountain destination is crucial. The interplay of the conditions, including the aspects of nature (vegetation, landscape, topography, scenery), qualities associated with recreational use (levels and types of use), and conditions provided by management (roads, developments, regulations), features in the Recreation Opportunity Spectrum framework to understand outdoor recreation (Clark & Stankey, 1979). This framework is mainly used to identify the types of recreation opportunities available in a setting and also to limit the development of specific areas at the destination (Joyce & Sutton, 2009; Xiao et al., 2018). All these factors act as essential aspects in the accessibility of mountaineering destinations.

While the conventional approach to research into the accessibility of mountaineering focuses primarily on Middleton's components (mentioned above) and describes the elements of a destination's accessibility (Allan, 1986; Gundersen et al., 2015; Price & Steiner, 2004), some scholars point out other elements. However, previous studies merely give details and mention only some aspects of accessibility in mountaineering destinations. For example, Maurer (2009) talks about the social (political) factors of accessibility, while others mention economic aspects (Huey, 2001; Nunes et al., 2013). Further studies consider the impact of climate change (Braun et al., 2009; Nunes et al., 2013) and the restrictions to accessibility due to weather conditions (Boyes et al., 1995; Purdie et al., 2015).

Due to the remoteness of most mountain locations and the difficulty of the terrain, access to mountainous regions is much more complex than for other tourism destinations; thus, a different approach to accessibility is needed than that for typical destinations (Middleton,

1994). Apollo (2017) notes that 'true accessibility for mountaineering is a combination of all the factors that shape it.' Hence, true accessibility of mountaineering incorporates (1) destination accessibility and (2) real access. Figure 2.2 illustrates the conceptual framework of true accessibility of mountaineering.

Destination accessibility is made up of two factors: *transport links* and *in situ services*. The term *transport links* relates to the existing transport connections and the possibilities to reach a destination. Transport links include flight, rail, road, water, and other alternative means of travel common to mountain tourism (such as paths, trails, and climbing routes). Munteanu (2010) points out that destination accessibility in terms of transport accessibility may be considered to include four aspects: spatial/territorial, economic, psychological, and social. Spatial/territorial (geographical) accessibility involves the physical distance between the point of origin and the destination. Economic accessibility determines the probable travel cost that the individual/group must pay. Psychological accessibility can be expressed by the effort required by an individual/group to reach the destination and describes the level of comfort in terms of, for example, perceived risk when travelling to or

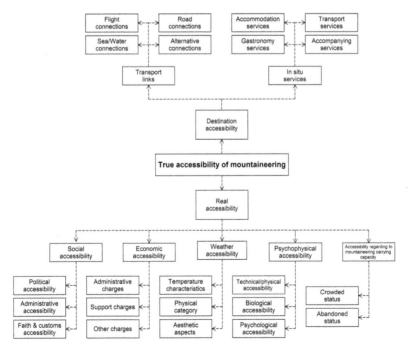

Figure 2.2 True accessibility of mountaineering (Apollo, 2017).

in the destination. Social accessibility is reflected by the age, the education level, and the social experiences of the individual/group.

The term *in situ services* (sometimes called the 'spatial element') covers all the necessary services (including infrastructure) to enable mountaineering tourism activities at a destination. These include hospitality services (incorporating accommodation and food services) and transport (e.g. porters and pack animals), all provided with a basic level of English and with accompanying services (Hall, 2005; Middleton, 1994; Middleton et al., 2009).

Mountaineering depends on and benefits from these services at all stages: the travel from a well-developed city to the last village accessible by road (first stage); the trek between the last village and the base camp (second stage); and the journey between the base camp and the ultimate mountaineering target (third stage). However, the most important services are those at the second and third stages. Table 2.2

Table 2.2 The structure of *in situ* services in developing countries at appropriate stages of travel (Apollo, 2017)

In situ service		*Stage of travel*		
		Stage II *Last village[a] to* *base camp*	*Stage III* *Base camp to* *target*	
Accommodation service		Hotel	Guesthouse, shelter, tent	Tent
Food service		Restaurant, shop	Restaurant, shop, self-catering	Self-catering
Transport service		Air (plane, helicopter), land (car, bus, 4WD)	Porters, pack animals	Porters
Accompanying service	Technical	Electrical grid, sanitary sewer	Electrical grid	Not available
	Social	Pharmacy, hospital, bank, public, administration, security services	Ambulatory	Not available
	Telecommunication	GSM	GSM, satellite connection	Satellite connection

a The last village (settlement) refers to the last place which can be reached by road; any further part of the route must be made on foot.

shows the structure of *in situ* services at appropriate stages of a trip in developing Global South countries.

Real accessibility (physical accessibility) comprises the conditions that must be fulfilled to allow physical contact with a tourist attraction (von Rohrscheidt, 2010). In short, even if the first factors (transport and *in situ* services) are met, real access to an attraction may be possible only under certain conditions. Hence, in mountaineering, *real accessibility* has five main aspects: social, economic, weather, psychophysical accessibility, and accessibility relating to mountaineering carrying capacity.

Social accessibility (social factors), in terms of accessibility to a mountain region, concerns three main areas of potential restriction: political (e.g. border regions, regions in conflict), administrative (e.g. temporary or a total ban on climbing), and faith and customs (e.g. sacred mountains, gender restrictions).

Areas with limited accessibility, either through sheer distance from the country's capital and developed cities or because of natural obstacles like mountains, often serve as geographic features that define the natural borders of a country (Diener & Hagen, 2012). Hence, some border regions are inaccessible to tourists (Timothy, 2002). Various conflicts, including geopolitical issues and, for example, the presence of terrorist organisations in the region, can also influence mountaineering by making mountain ranges or their parts inaccessible for mountaineering activities (consider, for example, mountain warfare around the world or the Shining Path in Peru).

Some mountainous areas have restrictions to accessibility resulting from an administrative decision. The main reasons for these restrictions and bans on mountaineering tourism are linked to environmental and religious issues. Climbing bans are temporarily introduced in order to protect vegetation or nesting birds in many mountain areas (the Algersdorfer Wald or the Stadeltenne in Frankenjura, Germany, for instance). An excellent example of the introduction of an administrative ban is the ban imposed at Mount Kailash (6,638 m) in 2001. Mount Kailash is a sacred mountain in four religions: Bön, Buddhism, Hinduism, and Jainism. In 2001 the Chinese government granted a permit for a Spanish team to climb the peak. However, after international backlash (including from climbers' organisations) and protests by those from the various faiths, the administration of the People's Republic of China decided to ban all attempts to climb the mountain.

Many other mountains of the world are known for their sanctity. Mount Kii (1,914 m) and Mount Fuji (3,776 m) in Japan; Mount Sinai (2,285 m) in Egypt; Mount Coropuna (6,425 m), Mount Ausangate (also

Auzangate, Quechua: Awsanqati) (6,384 m), and the Cinajara or Sinaqara glacier (5,471 m) in Peru; and the Llullaillaco volcano (2,344 m) in Argentina are the best examples of this form of spirituality. Thus, some of these retain a ban from mountaineering activity in the name of faith. Even if they are related to religion, some other restrictions come from customs, including bans based on gender. Mount Fuji is one of the three sacred mountains of Japan (the others being Mount Tate – 3,015 m; Mount Haku – 2,702 m) for followers of Shintoism, and, until 1868, it was forbidden for women to access the mountain (note: females are still banned from access to Mount Omine – 1,719 m). These kinds of restrictions can be found even today. An example is the Autonomous Monastic State of the Holy Mountain (autonomous territory of Hellenic Republic), with its highest peak Mount Athos (2,030 m), which has a prohibition on entry for women (Ring et al., 1994). These restrictions to accessibility, in some situations, make mountaineering activity practically impossible.

Economic accessibility is conditional upon the individual tourist's financial situation and is determined by the fees and costs associated with travel, permits, equipment, and expedition costs. In today's world this reaches tens of thousands of US dollars.

While the equipment used for hillwalking in an outdoor setting (trekking) has not changed significantly in recent decades, climbing equipment has been modernised, and hi-tech companies manufacture durable, lightweight, waterproof but breathable climbing equipment. However, even though the cost of proper mountaineering (climbing) equipment may come to approximately US$10,000, once purchased, the equipment will serve for many years, while fees need to be borne for each trip. Mountaineers are permitted access to attractions only after paying the required fee. Restrictions that relate to fees may occur on different levels: administrative (e.g. climbing permit or entry fee), support (e.g. climbing or trekking agency fee, rubbish disposal fee), and other charges (e.g. porters, guide fee, transport to the mountain).

While analysing the prices of services during specific stages of the destination lifecycle it was noticed that at first prices rise and then later they drop (Buhalis, 2000). However, mountaineering costs only increase (Attarian, 2001; Kreck et al., 2000; Nyaupane, 2015). Adventure tourism is an expensive activity, and typically wealthy tourists have limited time; hence, there is a push to squeeze as much experience into as short a time as possible (Beedie & Hudson, 2003). This is why individuals more often use paid climbing or trekking agencies to organise their expeditions, which in turn leads to an increase in the number of agencies. For example, in Nepal over a period of 25 years, the number of agencies rose from about two dozen to over 400, a nearly

17-fold increase (Bhattarai et al., 2005). Through this dramatic growth, a commercial approach has been introduced, and as all the stakeholders of mountaineering tourism, including governments, administrations, and trekking agencies, aim to make a profit, this inevitably leads to an increase in the costs associated with mountaineering tourism (Bardecki & Wrobel, 2015; Marek & Wieczorek, 2015; Savage & Torgler, 2015; Stewart, 2012). There is no doubt that this trend will remain.

It must be noted that some mountain areas are only accessible by using specialised agencies. For example, to climb Antarctica's highest peak – Mount Vinson (4,892 m) – the cost comes to at least US$40,000. A considerable portion of this amount is affected by Punta Arenas' flight prices to Patriot Hills and then on to Mount Vinson Base Camp. There is a similar situation with the highest peak in Papua New Guinea's Mount Puncak Jaya (4,884 m). The island of New Guinea, according to scholars (Johnson, 2004) and some climbers, Reinhold Messner, for example (see Apollo, 2014; Marek & Wieczorek, 2015), belongs to the continent of Australia (New Guinea, the country of Australia, Timor, smaller islands, and the continental shelf). Thus, the highest point on the continent is Mount Puncak Jaya (located on the island of New Guinea), and it is included in the Seven Summits peak-bagging challenge (Mount Kosciuszko replaces it in another version). Although climbing Mount Puncak Jaya is increasingly popular, it is hidden in the jungle of mountains, and access is quite challenging. Demanding trekking through dense jungle crossing tribal lands and difficulties obtaining several permits are among the main challenges. Due to the above circumstances, access is only possible through various adventure tourism agencies for at least US$12,000 (averaged data come from the ten most popular agencies as of 2019).

Thus, considering the examples above, the economic accessibility of mountaineering plays an important role even today, and perhaps it will remain the most critical element in the real accessibility of mountaineering in the future. The costs may reach a point that prevents many tourists from accessing the attractions, thus determining their availability.

Meteorological conditions are another factor that could significantly affect the success of an expedition (Savage & Torgler, 2015). *Weather accessibility* is based on the existence of optimal meteorological conditions for mountaineering. Changing meteorological elements affect the weather of mountains (well described by Barry [2008]), and thus they affect both the convenience and, often, the mere accessibility of mountaineering activity. Weather conditions also undergo dramatic changes over relatively short periods of time in mountain regions, which directly affects mountaineering success (Pomfret, 2006). However, given enough determination and patience, it is possible to climb almost any peak at any time of year. Considering the above-mentioned economic aspects of mountaineering (mountaineering costs) most mountaineers wish to maximise their success by picking the most favourable season (Soles & Powers, 2003). The world's mountain systems have seasonal variation, and usually climbers choose favourable periods (see Section 2.5., 'Meteorological determinants of the mountain climate and the seasonality of mountaineering activity') in which weather conditions will be more or less favourable for mountaineering (climbing seasons). There are two key seasons in mountaineering – summer and winter. The best conditions for mountaineering characterise the summer season. In the winter, a mountaineer is exposed to both extreme weather conditions (such as extreme temperatures, winds, freezing, avalanches, reduced daylight hours) and complex logistics (lack of *in situ* services that are available only in the summer season, lack of other teams for support, uncertainty of rescue). Although this division of summer and winter seasons applies only to areas outside the tropics, it has been adopted for all massifs worldwide to suit the needs of the mountain communities. Thus, the summer climbing season refers to both the dry season (which occurs in some regions between the tropics – Northern Andes, for example) and the periods before and after the monsoons (that occur in areas covered by monsoon winds, such as the Himalayas). Since the labels for climbing seasons (summer and winter) do not match with calendar seasons, we suggest calling the season with the most favourable conditions for summiting a peak the 'prime climbing season'. Table 2.3 illustrates the prime climbing seasons for the famous mountain peaks.

According to De Freitas (2001, 2003), the complex relationship between the meteorological conditions in the environment and the degree of joy from the outdoor pursuit of recreational activity may be seen as a function of local conditions. The human response to climate is essentially a matter of perception, except for temperature.

By using the 'facets of tourism climate' from De Freitas (2001, 2003), some limitations to accessibility caused by weather may be included. As such, listed among the 'facets of tourism climate' are temperature and its impact on the body, actual meteorological conditions (e.g. precipitation, snow cover, wind, solar radiation), and aesthetic weather conditions, such as overcast skies, visibility, and daylight hours. Favourable weather conditions are essential for mountaineering itself and play a role in scaling and travelling to mountains. However, weather elements may make the actual journey to a mountain difficult. Many mountain regions are reached by aeroplane or helicopter; weather conditions

Table 2.3 Prime climbing seasons

	January	February	March	April	May	June	July	August	September	October	November	December
Denali					░	░	░					
Vinson Massive	░										░	░
Aconcagua	░	░									░	░
Patagonia	░	░	░								░	░
Mount Kosciuszko	░	░	░	░	░	░	░	░	░	░	░	░
Bhutan Himalaya				░	░				░	░		
Cordillera Real (Bolivia)					░	░	░	░				
Baffin Mountains				░	░	░	░					
Cascade Range (Canada)						░	░	░	░			
Rocky Mountains (Canada)						░	░	░				
Saint Elias Mountains					░	░	░					
Tierra del Fuego	░	░									░	░
Tibet					░	░			░	░		
Colombian Andes	░	░					░	░				░
Cordillera Real (Ecuador)	░	░				░	░				░	░
Mont Blanc						░	░	░	░			
Watkins Range (Greenland)					░	░	░					
Garhwal Himalaya (India)					░	░			░	░		

(Continued)

January February March April May June July August September October November December

Puncak Jaya
Tien Shan
Trans-Mexican
   Volcanic Belt
Altai Mountains
High Atlas
Nepal Himalaya
   (e.g. Everest)
South Alps
Scandinavian
   Mountains
Lahaul Himalaya
Cordillera Blanca
Tatra Mountains
Caucasus (e.g.
   Elbrus)
Julian Alps
Pamir
Kilimanjaro
Taurus
   Mountains
Ruwenzori

must be excellent at the departure point and also at the place of arrival. Examples to highlight this include departure from Talkeetna and arrival at Kahiltna Glacier Base Camp for Denali in the Alaska Range; departure from Mount Cook Village and arrival at Grand Plateau for Mount Cook, Southern Alps; and departure from Kathmandu and arrival at Lukla to reach Mount Everest in the Himalayas.

Furthermore, weather conditions are also responsible for the quality (stability) of the mountain landscape and the mountaineer's safety. While falling rock and landslide hazards are related to geology (Clague & Stead, 2012), the relationships between the conditions of falling rock (or frequent landslides) and rainfall (see Dahal & Hasegawa, 2008) and freeze-thaw (see Noetzli et al., 2003) have been clearly established.

Meteorological conditions determine mountaineering activity, and therefore mountaineers are enticed to specific regions at certain times of the year. For example, warm, dry weather in summer would encourage participation in rock climbing. In contrast, warm weather in winter would discourage mountaineers from ice climbing due to melting ice and the risk of avalanche (Pomfret, 2006). Thus, climate change, which is well-documented in mountain regions (Elsasser & Bürki, 2002; Heather, 2013; Morrison & Pickering, 2013; Scott, 2006; Scott et al., 2007), may influence the choice of mountaineering destination (Purdie et al., 2015; Richardson & Loomis, 2004; Ritter et al., 2012) or at least modify the selection to a new range of outdoor activities (Elsasser & Bürki, 2002; Perry & Smith, 1996; Scott, 2006). In fact, in some places, this trend is already evident. For example, Kaenzig et al. (2016) report that the Chacaltaya glacier (5,400 m), famous since 1939 as the highest ski slope in the world, has instead become a trekking destination for tourists since 2005. Mountaineering and hiking may provide compensation for reduced skiing, and thus certain mountain regions may remain attractive destinations (Beniston, 2006). However, in the near future, some types of mountaineering activity, such as ice or grass climbing, will completely disappear from some mountain ranges. This has already happened in many mountain ranges, and some climbing routes used in the past are not even considered today. The best examples are the poorer conditions of ice climbing routes on Kilimanjaro (for a route description, see Salkeld & Bonington, 1998) or the inaccessible route on Siula Grande (6,344 m), a well-known mountain from Simpson's famous book *Touching the Void* (1988).

Thus, as weather sensitivity increases, mountaineering may only be possible during a short period each year (prime climbing season). However, even in a season with good conditions, a dramatic change in the weather may directly affect a mountaineer's success. Climate change, which affects weather accessibility, may also influence the behaviour (activity) of mountaineers and their choice of travel destination.

Psychophysical accessibility refers to the mountaineer's capabilities and mental well-being. The chosen destination and the mountaineering activity (climbing a summit or trekking around a mountain) must be within the participant's technical, physical, biological, and psychological limits. On high mountains, all kinds of routes (hiking, trekking, or climbing) require technical skills and physical and psychological preparation. It should be noted that even hiking or trekking at high elevations can be exhausting, even if the level of challenge and the grade of difficulty appear easy.

To determine whether a route will suit one's technical abilities, grades of climbing difficulty are used (see Section 2.3). The most famous system worldwide is the International Mountaineering and Climbing Federation's UIAA scale. The UIAA scale uses Roman numerals and was initially intended to run from I (most accessible – trekking or hiking) to VI (hardest – serious, extreme climbing). However, as with all other grading systems, improvements to climbing standards have led to the system being open-ended, and currently the most demanding climbs are graded XII− (Schöffl et al., 2011).

In contrast to the potential to improve one's technical and physical accessibility (limitations), biological adaptability to high altitudes is something that cannot be significantly changed. Some mountaineers can adjust, and others cannot. However, even when a mountaineer can adapt to high altitudes, the human body is only fully adaptable up to 5,300 m above sea level (Ward, 1975), while the potential risk of acute mountain sickness (AMS) can occur at just over 2,500 m (Luks et al., 2014; Vardy et al., 2006). The problems of high-altitude physiology and the process of adaptation and acclimatisation are well described in the literature (see West et al., 2012).

Although psychological limitations mainly refer to the ability to climb and the activity itself, they are also indirectly linked to anxiety (see Ryn 1988). In their research in Pamir, Lesiecka et al. (2012), as cited in Ryn (2016), verify that the level of anxiety (or fear) is closely connected to altitude. The level of fear increases with altitudes ranging from 700 to 4,100 m, and then after acclimatisation, it disappears. However, above 4,100 m, the severity of fear remains at a constant level. The authors identify fear as one of the axial symptoms of AMS. Both fear and joy have been proposed as core emotions evoked by mountaineering (Pomfret, 2006). However, fear is dominant during climbing activities (Ewert, 1985; Faullant et al., 2011; Ryn, 1988; Williams et al., 1978). Faullant et al. (2011) empirically confirm that 'mountaineers experience

joy and fear, and both of these basic emotions are important to the cus-
tomers' experience and their resulting satisfaction. While joy increases
satisfaction with a mountaineering tour, the opposite is true for fear.'
Fear is not a protagonist but represents a stage that can be recognised
and transcended (Brymer & Schweitzer, 2012). From an evolutionary
perspective, fear is related to survival (Ewert, 1985). Participants in extreme sports embrace fear, claim that fear is a 'friend', and once the
ability to recognise and invite a relationship with fear is learnt, fear
can be experienced as transformational (Brymer & Schweitzer, 2012).
However, not all kinds of fear that accompany mountaineering activity have been sufficiently understood, such as the well-known situation
in which all of the elements for climbing are in place but the climber
cannot function because of a psychological factor. This lack of trust in
one's abilities may also occur during trekking or hiking.

For these reasons, when selecting a destination (for hiking, trekking, or climbing), tourists must rely on their own experience and consider their personal limitations. The most common cause of failure
and related accidents in the mountains is the overestimation of capability, or 'bad judgment syndrome'. For example, if a climbing route
or target turns out to be too challenging, participants will be too slow
(physically) or unable to adapt (e.g. in the case of acclimatisation to
low atmospheric pressure) or suffer a temporary or permanent lack of
faith in his or her capabilities. Such factors are connected to the psychological well-being of a mountaineer (Lischke et al., 2001; Musa &
Thirumoorthi, 2015; Schussman et al., 1990; Trayers, 2004). Technical,
physical, biological, and psychological accessibilities are, in combination, one of the most important factor for real accessibility to mountaineering in all mountainous areas.

Accessibility relating to carrying capacity refers to congestion in
mountain areas and is strictly connected with mountaineering carrying capacity. According to the definition of the World Tourism Organization, which has been adopted in this study, carrying capacity
is the maximum number of people who may visit a tourist destination
at the same time, without destroying the physical, economic, and sociocultural environment and/or causing an unacceptable decrease in
the quality of visitors' satisfaction (Chamberlain, 1997; Middleton &
Hawkins, 1998). Tourism carrying capacity has been criticised both
from a conceptual and a practical point of view (Buckley, 1999; Lindberg et al., 1997); however, it is clearly defined in the case of mountaineering carrying capacity. On the entire vertical part of the climbing
route, there should strictly be only one climbing team (at most two
or three individuals) at any one time. Similarly, there should be only
one person on one section of a fixed rope or fixed line (common on

via ferrata routes). Also, mountain paths (trails), which are often way-marked with special signs (e.g. paint marks on the rocks or wooden signs, cairns), may be very steep and rocky. Above all, in the upper sections, paths may have a lot of exposure, which means that there is a high risk of injury in the event of a fall because of the incline of the terrain. Overloading climbing routes and trekking or hiking paths may bring about a severe risk of accidents. For example, a climber can accidentally detach a piece of rock (human-made rockfall), which may hit another climber below (a similar thing may happen on a steep path while traversing the slope of a mountain).

Three levels can be discerned in accessibility relating to carrying capability: crowded status (> carrying capacity), neutral status (= carrying capacity), and abandoned status (< carrying capacity). Neutral status does not influence the level of mountaineering accessibility because the number of mountaineers does not exceed the limit beyond which a mountain area may suffer from the adverse impacts of mountaineering. However, crowded status and its opposite – abandoned status – certainly have this influence.

Crowded status means that the number of mountaineers has exceeded the limit. Thus, all climbing routes or trekking trails are overloaded. This could seriously limit the availability of mountaineering activities. Too many people on one route or trail may force potential mountaineers to abandon that choice due to safety concerns (mentioned above) or a lack of willingness to wait for their turn. This kind of congestion may be observed in climbing, for example, on the classic ice gully Chèrè Couloir on Mont Blanc du Tacul's North Face or, in trekking, on the famous Yoshida Trail on Mount Fuji (3,776 m). Japan's highest peak is considered one of the country's preeminent tourism destinations and draws approximately 250,000–300,000 people every year to its summit during the mountaineering season, which runs from 1 July to 31 August.

However, overcrowding of trails or paths is not the only facet of carrying capacity that seriously restricts accessibility. In the case of mountaineering, the opposite of crowded status – abandoned status – may influence accessibility. Areas rarely visited by mountaineers will have more inadequate accessibility in terms of transport links and *in situ* services. This slows down the pace of reaching the region, and, if reaching the climbing site is most important (Buckley, 2012; Ewert & Hollenhorst, 1997), this may be a severe accessibility restriction. It is also worth mentioning that abandoned sites may not be marked adequately. While professional adventurers have no problems with loneliness (e.g. Steve House and his solo 42-hour climb on K7 in the Karakoram – discussed in House [2012]; Marek

Kaminski's lone trip to the South Pole – discussed in Kamiński [1998]), adventure tourists prefer places where they can meet others. This is probably connected to the fear of loneliness, survival skills, and a large number of people with the same position in the group blurring responsibility and promoting the approach that 'maybe the others will come up with something.' However, this needs to be empirically proven in the future.

2.4 Number of participants in mountaineering tourism

According to the definition of mountaineering tourism mentioned in Section 1.2., tourism in high-altitude mountain environments, which includes climbing, hiking, and trekking activities, is no longer the preserve of qualified and experienced mountaineers (Messerli & Ives, 1997; Nepal, 2008; Nepal & Mu, 2015). Recent studies highlight that the past few decades have brought a sharp increase in tourist numbers in mountain destinations (Marek & Wieczorek, 2015; Nepal, 2000; Zurick, 1992). This trend is due to three reasons: (1) increased fitness and physical abilities of participants in high-altitude-climbing tourism; (2) the evolution of mountaineering techniques (including climbing equipment, acclimatisation, belaying, and climbing style); (3) commercialisation (commodification) of high-mountain-climbing tourism (Apollo, 2014).

The volume of tourist traffic in high mountains can be estimated by checking the number of people belonging to alpine clubs or similar organisations. For example, according to the International Mountaineering and Climbing Federation, an international organisation associated with high-mountain climbing tourism clubs in 62 countries, it currently represents over 3 million people (Table 2.4).

Table 2.4 Membership numbers in clubs associated with UIAA

Continent	Country	Name of the associated federation	Number of members
North America	Canada	The Alpine Club of Canada	12,558
	Canada	Ecole Nationale d'Escalade du Québec	104
	Canada	Fédération Québécoise de la Montagne et de l'Escalade (FQME)	2,150
	Costa Rica	Federación Costarricense de Deportes de Montaña (FECODEM)	No data available

(*Continued*)

Continent	Country	Name of the associated federation	Number of members
	USA	The American Alpine Club	16,500
	USA	Alaskan Alpine Club	69
South America	Argentina	Federaciòn Argentina de Ski y Andinismo (FASA)	315
	Brazil	Confederação Brasileira de Montanhismo e Escalada (CBME)	1,658
	Chile	Federación de Andinismo de Chile	2,000
Europe	Andorra	Federació Andorrana de Muntanyisme	699
	Armenia	Armenian Alpine Club	28
	Austria	Verband Alpiner Vereine Österreichs	650,000
	Azerbaijan	Air and Extreme Federation of Azerbaijan	4,124
	Belgium	Climbing and Mountaineering Belgium (CMBEL-KBF)	13,641
	Bosnia and Herzegovina	Mountaineering Union of Bosnia – Herzegovina	6,100
	Bulgaria	Bulgarian Climbing and Mountaineering Federation	247
	Croatia	Croatian Mountaineering Association – Hrvatski Planinarski Savez	11,094
	Cyprus	Mountaineering and Climbing Federation of Cyprus	300
	Czech Republic	Czech Mountaineering Federation – Cesky Horolezecky Svaz	11,620
	Czech Republic	Czech Mountain Leader Association – Český spolek horských průvodců	72
	Denmark	Dansk Bjergklub – Danish Alpine Club	1,087
	Denmark	Danish Climbing Federation	6,474
	Finland	Finnish Climbing Association	3,201
	France	Fédération française des clubs alpins et de montagne	82,815
	Georgia	Mountaineering and Climbing Association of Georgia	301
	Germany	Deutscher Alpenverein	1,131,658
	Greece	Hellenic Federation of Mountaineering and Climbing	6,460

Continent	Country	Name of the associated federation	Number of members
	Hungary	Magyar Hegy – és Sportmászó Szövetség – Hungarian Mountaineering and Sport Climbing Federation (MHSSz)	479
	Ireland	Mountaineering Ireland	11,554
	Italy	Club Alpino Italiano	307,069
	Italy	Unit Member International Skyrunning Federation	No data available
	Italy	Alpenverein Südtirol (AVS)	62,640
	Jordan	Jordan Tourism	No data available
	Kosovo	Kosovo Mountaineering and Alpinist Federation	1,045
	Liechtenstein	Liechtensteiner Alpenverein	2,753
	Lithuania	Lithuanian Mountaineering Association	130
	Luxembourg	FLERA	491
	Macedonia	Macedonian Mountain Sport Federation	395
	Monaco	Club Alpin Monégasque (CAM)	10
	Netherlands	Royal Dutch Mountaineering and Climbing Club	58,697
	Norway	Norwegian Alpine Club – Norsk Tindeklub	657
	Norway	Norges Klatreforbund – The Norwegian Climbing Federation	19,860
	Poland	Polish Mountaineering Association	3,170
	Portugal	Clube Nacional de Montanhismo	98
	Portugal	Federação de Campismo e Montanhismo de Portugal – UPD	670
	Portugal	Federação Portuguesa de Montanhismo e Escalada (FPME)	580
	Portugal	Clube de Actividades de Ar Livre	561
	Romania	Clubul Alpin Român – Romanian Alpine Club	No data available
	Russia	Russian Mountaineering Federation	1,300
	Serbia	Mountaineering Association of Serbia – Planinarski Savez Srbije	1,120

(*Continued*)

Continent	Country	Name of the associated federation	Number of members
	Slovakia	Slovak Mountaineering Union JAMES – Slovensky Horolezecky Spolok JAMES	4,522
	Slovenia	Alpine Association of Slovenia	54,574
	Spain	Federación Española de Deportes de Montaña y Escalada (FEDME)	108,145
	Spain	Centre Excursionista de Catalunya	4,400
	Spain	Euskal Mendizale Federazioa – Basque Mountaineering Federation	30,788
	Spain	Federació d'Entitats Excursionistes de Catalunya (FEEC)	38,324
	Sweden	Swedish Climbing Federation – Svenska Klätterförbundet (SKF)	8,000
	Switzerland	Schweizer Alpen Club (SAC)	142,787
	Switzerland	Vereinigung der Akademischen Alpen – Clubs der Schweiz	428
	Switzerland	International Federation of Mountain Guides Associations (IFMGA/ UIAGM/IVBV)	6,000
	Turkey	Turkiye Dagcilik Federasyonu – Turkish Mountaineering Federation	19,990
	Turkey	ZIRVE MOUNTAINEERING CLUB	1,750
	Ukraine	Ukrainian Mountaineering and Climbing Federation	1,698
	United Kingdom	British Mountaineering Council	52,602
	United Kingdom	The Alpine Club	1,529
Africa	South Africa	The Mountain Club of South Africa	4,127
Asia	Bangladesh	Bangladesh Mountaineering Federation	49
	China	Chinese Mountaineering Association	13,500
	Hong Kong	China Hong Kong Mountaineering and Climbing Union	4,980
	India	Indian Mountaineering Foundation	108

Continent	Country	Name of the associated federation	Number of members
	India	Himalayan Mountaineering Institute	144
	India	Nehru Institute of Mountaineering	62
	Indonesia	Indonesia Sport Climbing and Mountaineering Federation	No data available
	Iran	I.R. Iran Mountaineering and Sport Climbing Federation	20,000
	Israel	Israel Climbers' Club (Former Israeli Alpine Club)	424
	Japan	Japan Mountaineering Association	43,000
	Korea	Corean Alpine Club	836
	Korea	Korean Alpine Federation	1,000
	Malaysia	National Adventure Association of Malaysia	60
	Mongolia	Mongolian National Mountaineering Federation	200
	Nepal	Nepal Mountaineering Association	1,250
	Pakistan	Alpine Club of Pakistan	100
	Sri Lanka	National Mountaineering and Climbing Association Sri Lanka	No data available
	Taiwan	Chinese Taipei Alpine Association	2,318
	Taiwan	Chinese Taipei Mountaineering Association	300
Oceania	New Zealand	New Zealand Alpine Club, Inc.	3,504
Total			3,010,053

The actual number of mountaineers is probably much higher. For example, in the USA alone, it is estimated to be 2.6 million people (Outdoor Foundation, 2016), which is 150 times the number of American Alpine Club members (16,500 members). Thus, the number of participants in high-mountain-climbing tourism may reach a dozen or even several dozen million on a global scale. An estimated value of tens of millions is closer to reality, especially if we consider pilgrimage traffic to places located in high mountains.

2.5 Meteorological determinants of the mountain climate and the seasonality of mountaineering activity

The decisive factor for human activity on earth is the geographical environment, and above all – as the French philosopher Montesquieu (1777) shares in *The Spirit of Laws* – climate, because it exerts a massive influence on the psyche of humans, and indirectly also on customs, laws, and social systems. Despite many controversies related to Montesquieu's work – albeit a development of the views of ancient thinkers (Strabo, Hippocrates) – the concept that 'climate power is the first power in the world' is difficult to disagree with in relation to extremely challenging mountain conditions, in which all activities are subordinate to the climate.

Makowski (2006) prefers to focus on the environmental conditions of the observed phenomena (e.g. forms of settlement, forms of management, poverty, and economic backwardness) and not their environmental (natural) causes. One can agree or disagree with the following thesis: the settlement area of mountain areas is limited by bioclimatic phenomena that define its boundaries. However, high-altitude-climbing activity is entirely subordinate to the climate, and it will undoubtedly remain Montesquieu's first authority in this activity. Climate, defined as many years (at least 30) of all phenomena and meteorological conditions, shapes the schedule of mountain expeditions. The most favourable season for mountaineers is, therefore, the period with the best weather conditions in a given area – the best for mountaineering, of course. Therefore, the conditions must be optimal and, for example, cannot be either too cold (bringing the risk of frostbite) or too warm (bringing the risk of avalanches).

The climatic diversity that characterises individual mountain regions of the world leads to confusion about their typology. The modern version of W. Koppen's climate classification identifies the mountain climate with the letter H (in German: Hochgebirge; in English: High mountains). A general definition of the mountain climate has never been, and probably will not be, created because individual mountains generate their own climate, which is strongly dependent on the properties of the climatic zone in which they are located. However, it is possible to indicate specific features that characterise this type of climate: sudden and numerous weather changes, the presence of sizeable daily temperature amplitudes, abundant precipitation, and strong winds (often hurricane winds). The mountain climate is determined by several meteorological elements: radiation, temperature, air pressure, precipitation, and wind. All of them are somewhat related to the location on the globe because modern geographers conventionally treat latitude as the main climate-creating factor. It is clear that latitude as such does not affect climate – it is energy (insolation) and not angle (latitude) that is the major factor in the earth's climate and spatial variability.

The amount of solar **radiation** reaching the surface of the earth increases with altitude and is directly dependent on the atmosphere's permeability. However, the calculation of radiation level is exceptionally complicated, mainly because of formulas that assume a horizontal surface of the earth. An increase in altitude changes the thickness of the atmosphere, which is directly related to the reduction of its mass and leads to greater permeability. Sauberer and Dirmhirn (1965) show that the value of total solar radiation increases with increasing altitude, based on measurements carried out in the Austrian Alps at an altitude of 200 m and 3,000 m. For the given amounts it increased by 21 per cent in January and by 33 per cent in December. The decreased thickness of the atmosphere and the smaller volume of water vapour and aerosols reduce the dispersion of visible and ultraviolet radiation. The effect of this phenomenon is a dark blue, sometimes navy, sky colour. Reiter and Munzert (1982), based on five years of observations in the Northern Alps, prove that the total ultraviolet radiation reaching the earth's surface at an altitude of 3,000 m is (as much as) 1.4 times in January and 1.5 times in June higher than at an altitude of 700 m.

The supply of radiant energy from the sun depends on the amount of time between sunrise and sunset. Seasonal changes in day length and associated solar radiation are usually slight at low latitudes (Kilimanjaro 3° 04″ S; Puncak Jaya 4° 05″ S). On the other hand, in the polar zones, the difference between the length of the day and night in the extreme periods of the year is already significant. At the summit of Mount Denali (6,190 m) in Alaska (63° 05′ N), during the calendar summer, the day lasts more than 20 hours, and it shortens to just over 5 hours during the winter. The radiant energy's insolation value significantly decreases with increasing latitude, which means that towards the poles, the range of the tree line and the snow line also decreases. This means that the alpine vegetation layer (above the forest line) and the levelling layer (eternal snow) are lower in the mountains at high latitudes than in the tropics.

Not all radiant energy reaching the earth's surface is absorbed. Part of it is reflected and thus not utilised in heating the earth. The ratio of reflected incident energy is determined by the albedo value (range 0–1). The higher the albedo value, the less energy is absorbed by a given surface. Its value depends on the ground cover, which varies from season to season in the mountains (with alpine meadows in summer, and snow and ice in winter). For example, the change in the albedo in the Caucasus was 0.28 at an altitude of 2,130 m (rock rubble) and up to 0.74 at an altitude of 5,300 m (naval zone). It is evident that direct sunlight increases with altitude. Research conducted in the Alps shows that at heights of over 3,000 m, total solar radiation increases between 7 and 10 per cent for every 1,000 m in the absence of cloud cover and between 9 and 11 per cent with full sky coverage. In the high mountains above the border of eternal snow, the beam of direct radiation is scattered and changed in many directions due to repeated reflection from snow dust and often uneven ice and snow cover. The exposure, which is highly variable in high mountain ranges, plays an essential role in the irradiation of slopes. For example, at latitude 50° N, on slopes of 45°, there are significant differences in the inflow of solar radiation depending on their north or south exposure. The shaded northern slopes can only receive diffuse radiation. Largely for this reason, snow cover stays longer on the northern wall faces in the Northern Hemisphere.

The relationship between change in air **temperature** and altitude is one of the hallmarks of the mountain atmosphere. It was explained in the 18th century by the Swiss physicist Horace Bénédict de Saussure, who is considered to be the first mountain meteorologist and the father of modern meteorology. Under the conditions of a certain air mass, the air temperature in the mountains is a function of altitude, exposure, and topography. The spatial temperature distribution in the mountain atmosphere is very strongly related to the type of substrate, which has uneven absorption of solar energy due to the different albedo values. The heat energy absorbed during the day is radiated out during the night. The size of the heat flux depends mainly on the size of the thermal gradient and the substrate's physical properties. The latter depends on the heat capacity of the ground, its humidity or air content, and heat transmission. Particular examples of the substrate are glaciers or water surfaces, which by heating and cooling in a specific way, lead to numerous perturbations in the thermal balance of the substrate.

In meteorology, constants have been introduced describing the value of the temperature gradient in the free atmosphere, which, depending on the water vapour content in the air, are defined as a dry-adiabatic gradient (0.5°C/100 m), moist-adiabatic gradient (0.98°C/100 m), and the actual temperature gradient (0.6°C/100 m). In the given gradients, however, it is necessary to consider a specific modification, taking place not only under the influence of air circulation but also due to thermal inversion, which often occurs in mountainous areas. Both these factors clearly affect the average monthly temperature values. Alisow et al. (1952) describe the phenomenon of thermal inversion in the inter-mountain valleys in Siberia, where the average temperature in February in Verkhoyansk (120 m) was 8.3°C lower than at the observation point 900 m higher at the Siemieniowska Mine.

Deviations from the above-mentioned rate of gradient change also depend on the seasonality (daily, annual) and the climatic zone in which the area is located. Many researchers point out that determining the vertical temperature gradient in mountains is impossible, mainly due to the varied topography and the unusual air circulation dynamics. The air in the mountain atmosphere is also easier to mix than in the free atmosphere. The main reasons for the warming of the mountain atmosphere are the heat flow from the ground, the supply of latent heat of condensation in the air, and the formation of clouds, often of high water capacity. The exception is ground covered with eternal snow, mentioned earlier in the book, which has a cooling effect on the atmosphere. The temperature was measured at various altitudes (4,700–7,000 m) in the Tian Shan mountain system and compared to the results obtained in the free atmosphere. The results showed that in these (snow-covered) areas the average temperature was 1.8°C lower than in the free atmosphere.

The value of the daily temperature amplitude decreases with increasing altitude. The magnitude of this change is strictly influenced by the latitude and the degree of continentalism in the mountain area. For example, the highest administrative capital in the world, located at latitude 16° S, La Paz (3,640 m), has very little annual variation in average monthly temperature values, while the capital of the Tibet Autonomous Region, Lhasa (3,656 m), located at a similar altitude above sea level (29° N), shows significant disproportions between the summer and winter seasons.

Rapid temperature change with altitude leads to the formation of climatic and plant floors, which are often given specific proper names. For example, in the tropics of Latin America, there are four floors: Tierra Caliente (hot zone), Tierra Templada (moderate zone), Tierra Fria (cold zone), and Tierra Helada (frost zone). Each of these floors has a specific, successive arrangement of vegetation.

At mid- to high-latitudes, January and June are thermally different months. However, January is not always the warmest month in all regions in the Northern Hemisphere. The proximity of the ocean or sea can affect the average temperature of the hottest month. A cold sea current or a summer monsoon causes a temperature shift of up to several degrees Celsius.

The relationship between altitude and atmospheric pressure was proven 300 years ago and is the most documented element that shapes the mountain climate. The pressure change with height in cool air is greater than in warm air, which means that isobaric surfaces at lower latitudes, in warm air, will be located higher. Prohaska (1970) explains that the subtropical atmosphere's pressure is approximately 15 hPa higher at an altitude of 3,000 m above sea level and about 20 hPa at an altitude of 5,000 m than at the exact altitudes in moderate latitudes (from the tropics to about 65° latitude). Air pressure is not to be confused with the oxygen content of the air. If the oxygen content in the atmosphere is 21 per cent at sea level, then on Ben Nevis (1,345 m), Mont Blanc (4,809 m), or Everest (8,848 m), it will also be 21 per cent, but at a lower pressure. The central role here is played by the partial pressure, which decreases proportionally with the decrease in atmospheric pressure. These dependencies show that at an altitude of 3,000 m above sea level, a person begins to experience problems with sufficient ventilation of the body. Without proper acclimatisation, at an altitude of 6,000 m above sea level there is a threat to life, which is associated with oxygen deficiency despite the constant content of approximately 21 per cent of oxygen in the breathing air. The reason lies in the aforementioned partial pressure of oxygen, which at sea level is approximately 160 mmHg (21 kPa) and, at an altitude of 6,000 m above sea level, only approximately 80 mmHg (10 kPa), half the pressure of that at sea level.

The variability of weather in the mountains is most often associated with the possibility of sudden and difficult-to-predict **precipitation**. In the mountain atmosphere, the physical processes that determine precipitation are comparable to those in the free atmosphere. However, several factors increase the frequency of their occurrence. Trepińska (2002) showed quantitative and qualitative factors influencing these differences. These are the water vapour content in the air, the level of water vapour condensation, the water of the clouds, the advection direction of moist air masses, and the speed of vertical air movements. The above factors, so characteristic of the mountain atmosphere, are isolated from the free atmosphere, which significantly increases their quantitative and qualitative factor.

The influence of latitude on the temperature regime has a certain influence on the rainfall characteristics. In the mountains above 4,000 m near the equator, snow can fall every day, regardless of the season. In contrast, mountains at middle and higher latitudes have a well-marked winter season. The amount of precipitation in the mountains depends mainly on the height of the measuring point above sea level. This claim, however, may not be considered correct in all cases. Morphological features (type of relief, slope exposure, chain direction or its surface area, etc.) that shape the mountain climate play a significant role. Sheltered from prevailing winds, mountain peaks may experience different rainfall, despite being in the same climatic zone.

The research clearly shows the high correlation of precipitation with the orography of the area. Due to the altitude, exposure, and relief, most of the world's great mountain ranges are considered significant climatic barriers – the orographic barriers. A perfect example of the ongoing deformation of atmospheric fronts is the Himalayas. By blocking the polar air masses moving south from Central Asia, the temperature in the winter months is much higher in the southern part of the chain. The Himalayas also block the warm and humid air from the south–north direction during the summer monsoons, providing high rainfall on the mountains' southern slopes. Mighty mountain ranges, being a significant obstacle to the advection of rain-bearing air masses, lead to significant disproportions in the amount of precipitation on the opposite slopes (windward and leeward). An example of the formation of extremely high rainfall from the windward side (Homer Tunnel, Fiordland – 6,233 mm) and the orographic dry area from the leeward side (Alexandra, Otago – 230 mm) is the Southern Alps in New Zealand.

Moving air masses (**wind**) show a much lower velocity near the earth's surface (friction) than in the free atmosphere. Therefore, the wind speed shows a positive correlation with the distance from the earth's surface, meaning an increase in altitude. The research by Wahl (1953) carried out in the Alps clearly shows that the wind speed at the peak of the summit is twice as low as that at the same height in the free atmosphere. Despite this, wind speeds recorded in the mountains are among the highest on our planet. For many years, Mount Washington (1,917 m), the highest peak of the White Mountains (Appalachia Mountains), boasted a record speed. On 12 April 1934, the meteorological observatory recorded a wind speed of 372 km/h on its summit.

Mountains not only have extreme wind speeds but, most importantly, act as a topographic barrier that modifies the wind's direction in two ranges: horizontal and vertical. As Trepińska (2002) points out, the airflow modified by all landform forms, and depending on the morphological features (e.g. absolute altitude), can be perceived on a planetary, continental, regional, or local scale.

The anemological conditions in the mountains are characterised by a variety of air currents forced by the movement of air around and over the mountains, as well as in the narrowing created by their relief. Examples of mountain winds include katabatic winds (e.g. fen, bora), anabatic winds (forced by the orographic barrier), mountain-valley circulation (slope winds: valley winds during the day, mountain winds at night), glacial winds, and pass winds. Mountain winds have a large, often underestimated importance in shaping the mountain climate and, in a way, the landscape. The warm and dry fen winds blowing from the mountains reach hurricane speeds, often exceeding 200 km/h.

For example, a halny (a warm windstorm that blows through the valleys) flowing from the southern slopes of the Tatra Mountains reached the highest speed of 300 km/h (in the night from 6 May to 7 May 1968). The consequence of the speeds achieved by mountain winds is significant loss of, or damage to, vegetation, windbreaks, and inhabited spaces (buildings). This speed is also accompanied by a drastic change in temperature in the valleys. In this respect, the undisputed record holder is the snow devourer (Chinook) blowing from the eastern slopes of the Rocky Mountains. On 22 January 1943, in just 2 minutes, it increased the temperature in Spearfish (South Dakota) by 27°C (-20°C to $+7^{\circ}$C), and on 15 January 1972, within 24 hours, it changed the temperature in Loma (Montana) by 58°C (from -48°C to 9°C).

As shown earlier in the chapter, mountain ranges have periods (seasons) in which the weather (meteorological) conditions are more or less favourable to climbing. Climbing and expedition seasons are generally divided into summer and winter (see Section 2.3). The dry season in intertropical climates is the de facto climatic winter, which is the period of the highest mountain activity due to the stable weather. Intensive rainfall during the calendar summer (rainy season) may make it impossible to undertake any mountain activities (due to avalanche risk) or make it impossible to get uphill (because of impassable paths or broken bridges on mountain rivers). For example, the calendar summer in the Higher Himalayas is an extremely unfavourable period for mountaineering activities, with heavy rain and snowfall. The summer climbing season there coincides with the calendar spring and autumn.

In order to standardise, the term 'prime climbing season' was introduced, which characterises the best (optimal) weather and snow conditions for high-mountain activity, when statistically the summit is reached by the most people. Hence, having a basic understanding of climatic conditions in mountain environments is a crucial skill for mountaineers. However, the evidence shows that few modern mountaineers are capable of 'weather work' (Allen-Collinson, 2018). Many contemporary mountaineers have little knowledge of weather, climate, and terrain and how they influence each other. Many are therefore often unable to interpret or forecast mountain weather conditions in challenging situations (Allen-Collinson et al., 2018).

Furthermore, climate change has a negative impact on mountaineering and makes the activity even riskier. According to the CREA Mont Blanc (the Research Centre for Alpine Ecosystems based in Chamonix), glaciers in the European Alps have lost 50 per cent of their volume since 1900, and temperatures have risen by 2°C over the 20th century (CREA Mont Blanc, 2015). As such, climate change may impact the attractiveness of a mountain destination, the safety of mountaineering due to the instability of climate, and an increase in high-magnitude weather events (e.g. heavy snow can lead to a number of safety problems like an avalanche; see, Hall, 2015; Harrison et al., 2005). Furthermore, the temperature, humidity, and precipitation shifts resulting from climate change may impact mountaineering destinations and route selection as well as mountaineering style (Mourey et al., 2019).

2.6 The human body and high-altitude environments exposure

Mountaineering tourism is accompanied by a number of physiological problems, particularly the body's adaptation to the changing conditions of the high-mountain environment. In high-altitude medicine, the term 'high altitude' refers to heights beyond 1,500 m above sea level (Figure 2.3). Areas classified as high (1,500–3,500 m), very high (3,500–5,500 m), and extremely high (over 5,500 m) are commonly identified (Gallagher & Hackett, 2004; Wilson et al., 2009). If at 1,500 m health complications related to high altitude have not arisen, the risk of developing one or more forms of acute altitude illness increases significantly from 2,500 m (Luks et al., 2010).

The high-mountain environment is an aggressive factor that can lead to the functional impairment of those exposed to it. It is counteracted by the body's adaptive mechanisms in terms of endurance and immunity and also through acclimatisation (Kiełkowska & Kiełkowski, 2003). Acclimatisation differs from adaptation, and the latter consists only of getting used to oxygen deficiency and the unpleasant symptoms associated with it (without physiological and morphological adaptation; see, Radwańska-Paryska & Paryski, 1995). The same approach to both concepts has often led to erroneous conclusions, particularly among high-mountain tourists, that repeated contact with altitude improves the possibilities for acclimatisation and the pace of acclimatisation (see West et al. 2012). Repeated visits to significant altitudes positively affect the human psyche as with experience in high-altitude environments – individuals become aware of their own limitations and capabilities for adaptation. The acclimatisation process is a physiological and morphological adaptation, and it is the same each time. It must be carried out every time one travels to a high-altitude mountain, and it cannot be skipped (Kowalewski & Kurczab, 1983). Among the harmful factors affecting the

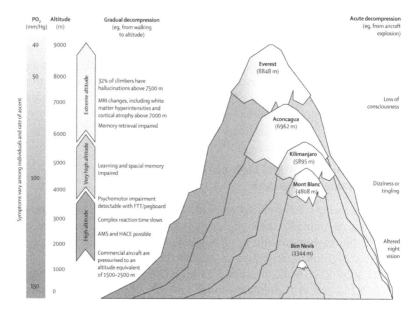

Figure 2.3 Neurological effects of atmospheric pressure drop with altitude (classified as high [1,500–3,500 m], very high [3,500–5,500 m], and extreme [>5,500 m]). AMS = acute mountain sickness. HACE = high-altitude cerebral edema. HAPE = high-altitude pulmonary edema. FTT = finger-tapping test (redrawn from Wilson at al., 2009).

human body exposed to a high-mountain environment, Kowalewski and Kurczab (1983) indicate (1) reduced atmospheric pressure and the associated decrease (with an increase in altitude) of oxygen partial pressure, (2) reduction of air humidity, (3) drop in air temperature, and (4) radiation.

In addition, these factors are exacerbated by the person's physical condition when they reach an extreme height, impacted by dehydration, hunger, or physical exhaustion (Szymczak, 2009b). Each of the elements mentioned above is of great importance, but the drop in air pressure with an increase in altitude is certainly the dominant factor. The importance of air pressure is clearly confirmed by numerous studies conducted in simulated conditions (hypobaric chambers), during which the only variable to which the body was exposed was extremely low atmospheric pressure (Pugh, 1962; Szymczak, 2009b; West et al., 2012). Chronic hypoxia (a condition in which the body or a region of the body is deprived of adequate oxygen supply at the tissue level) may be the cause of deterioration. The deterioration in high-mountain conditions is characterised by decreased appetite, weight loss and other resultant changes in body composition, cognitive impairment, decreased motivation and enthusiasm for further activity, and deteriorated sleep quality (Szymczak, 2009b; Weil, 2004). The acclimatisation process takes place at several physiological and morphological levels. In its first phase, precisely the same regulatory system operates, which manifests in all pressure conditions, when intense physical effort increases the body's demand for oxygen (Kowalewski & Kurczab, 1983). It causes an increase in lung ventilation, an acceleration of the heart rate, and increased blood pressure, which directly improves gas exchange. The increase in pressure in pulmonary blood vessels causes blood to enter the parts of the lungs that are not usually used at lowland level (West et al., 2012).

However, the processes described above will not occur properly if acclimatisation is not carried out at the appropriate pace. The suggested method for correct acclimatisation includes two primary recommendations: (1) above 3,000 m, do not climb more than 300^3 m in altitude difference per day and (2) take a rest every two to three days, which consists of spending two nights at the same altitude (Kowalewski & Kurczab, 1983). The best way to carry out acclimatisation is to climb higher and higher and to rest at lower camps – the so-called *saw tooth system*. Unfortunately, this rule is very rarely followed. This is mainly due to ignorance about the adaptation (acclimatisation) process and its pace and the desire to quickly achieve a goal or take advantage of good weather conditions. Frequent media reports on accidents in the mountains only confirm this thesis. The ignorance mentioned above is related to the common belief that the acclimatisation process should only be carried out when climbing the peaks at a height of 8,000 m or more.

Even adherence to all of the guidance for preparing the body to be at high altitude does not mean that the individual's overall fitness will not decrease (Dahal & Hasegawa, 2008). An increase in altitude always lowers a person's efficiency. It manifests, inter alia, in a decrease in the oxygen ceiling (VO2 max), meaning a decrease in the body's maximum ability to absorb oxygen. This decrease – the most frequently used indicator of respiratory efficiency – is already observed from 1,500 m above sea level. It progresses linearly by about 11 per cent for every 1,000 m, with only 20 per cent of the value observed at sea level at 8,000 m (Kiełkowska & Kiełkowski, 2003). Increasing the frequency of breathing – lung hyperventilation – increases the dehydration process in a dry high-mountain atmosphere, and the related energy consumption contributes to a decrease in physical performance. All this, combined with the drop in temperature and the increase in radiation, leads to a number of diseases and health disorders. Due to the physical effort and high amounts of energy spent adapting to the conditions, a person loses 0.5–1.5 kg of their mass during a week in high-mountain conditions (at an altitude of 5,800 m; see Pugh, 1962).

There is one more limitation of the acclimatisation process – even if the process is carried out correctly – and it concerns the maximum height to which the human body is able to completely adapt. Although the early studies of Wyss-Dunant (1953) estimated the altitude to be 7,000 m, in fact, this figure was too optimistic. Ward (1975) significantly lowered the altitude, indicating that the altitude limit to which complete acclimatisation is possible is approximately 5,300 m, although, as shown by the latest research by Szymczak (2009b), heights beyond 5,000 m above sea level can cause deterioration in the human body. For this reason, one can only speak of relative (partial) acclimatisation in the range of 5,300–7,000 m above sea level (Kowalewski & Kurczab, 1983). Ward (1975) calls the band between 7,000 and 7,800 m the adaptation time zone. Staying at an altitude above 7,800 m without an artificial supply of oxygen will inevitably lead to a physical and mental collapse of the system in a short time. The mechanisms responsible for adaptation processes cease, and the caloric balance is negative. After three to five days at this altitude, death occurs (Ryn, 1967). The belt above 7,800 m is referred to as the high-altitude death zone (Ward, 1975).

The process of acclimatisation varies from person to person; some adapt quickly, others slowly, and some show a complete lack of predisposition to being at high altitudes (Kiełkowska & Kiełkowski, 2003). In every respect, inadequate (too fast) acclimatisation is the most common cause of health complications, which can even lead to death from cold and radiation (Hackett & Roach, 2001). The most common diseases related to altitude include acute altitude sickness, altitude pulmonary edema, altitude cerebral edema, peripheral altitude edema, fluid in the alveoli, and retinal haemorrhage. Furthermore, other weather factors such as snow conditions most often lead to frostbite, hypothermia, or blindness, and exposure to the sun at high altitude can cause heat exhaustion, sunstroke, and sunburns. For a detailed description of the above diseases and their symptoms, prevention, and treatment measures, see, for example, Broadhurst and Smith (2008) and Szymczak (2009a).

Researchers highlight that the sudden transfer of a person from a coastal settlement to an 8,000-m summit can cause the immediate loss of consciousness (refer to aeronautic accidents, research conducted in pressure chambers) and, consequently, death (Davis et al., 2005;

Szymczak, 2009a; West et al., 2012). Therefore, gaining altitude during mountain activities requires time for the body to make a slow adaptation (the so-called acclimatisation). The acclimatisation process forces the mountaineering participant to stay in the alpine environment much longer than the distance alone would require. For example, looking only at the 50-km Machame Route leading to the summit of Kilimanjaro (5,895 m above sea level), the ascent and descent (base camp – summit – base camp) together usually take six days. However, the correct acclimatisation – following the guidelines of mountain medicine – should take a minimum of 12 days. Risking health and life, climbers usually limit this time to seven to eight days. During ascent to a summit of 8,000 m or above, the acclimatisation process may extend the time of ascent (staying in the massif) to over two months. Thus, the impact of mountaineering on the environment should be related to the number of participants and the time they spend in the mountainous environment.

2.7 Risks for mountaineers and environmental hazards in mountains

Mountain tourists have to deal with exposure to danger (objective and subjective; Apollo, 2021). The subjective risk is related to tourist imperfection (experience), which subjectively assesses the probability of certain phenomena occurring in the future. In contrast, the objective risk is the absolute form of uncertainty, which is related to the impossibility of predicting the development of certain phenomena (disasters like earthquakes or floods). Pröbstl-Haider et al. (2016) demonstrated that (subjective) risk-taking is influenced by three main factors: (1) the experience, frequency of participation, and commitment; (2) the perception of risky environmental conditions; and (3) the individual risk-related trade-off including information, the desired experience, and other given constraints such as time management or weather conditions. Mountains are also wild, rugged places that attract bad weather and contain objective dangers, such as exposure to extreme elemental conditions and loose rock, which make any mountain activities inherently risky and hazardous (Barry, 2008; Beedie & Hudson, 2003).

Furthermore, another characteristic of high-mountain environments, with the Himalayas as an excellent example, is the significant energy of all processes (large height differences – sculpture energy, convection, and active exchange of air masses – heat supply from below, cold air flow downwards), causing high dynamism of geological, geomorphological, hydrological, and climatic elements

(Apollo & Andreychouk, 2022). Thus, the risks and dangers of operating in such places become more significant, and the management response to this is expressed in the generation of rules designed to rationalise those dangers through appropriate preparation, planning, and performance (Beedie, 2003). Being a mere tourist is no longer acceptable, especially in such a risky environment where natural hazards occur often (Ziegler et al., 2021).

Based on the example of the Himalayas, Ziegler et al. (2021) developed a causal loop diagram to illustrate the relationship between leadership and the disaster management cycle. The disaster management cycle involves four main components:

Preparedness: Develop a satisfactory level of readiness to respond to any emergency situation. Necessary actions: preparedness plans, vulnerability assessment, emergency exercises, training, warning systems, emergency communications, evacuations plans and training, resource inventories, emergency personnel contact lists, mutual aid agreements, public information, education.

Mitigation: Eliminate or reduce the probability of disaster occurrence or reduce the effects of unavoidable disasters. Necessary actions: construction codes, vulnerability analyses updates, zoning and land-use management, usage regulations and safety codes, preventive healthcare, hazard reduction, public education.

Response: Provide immediate assistance to maintain life, improve health, and support the morale of the affected population. Necessary actions: search and rescue, evacuation, medical attention, provision of food and shelter, coordination/communication, rapid impact assessment.

Recovery: Conduct activities aimed at restoring livelihoods and infrastructure following a disaster, as well as learning from events to feed back into preparedness for the future. Necessary actions: restoration of vital life-support infrastructure, provision of temporary housing, dissemination of public information, provision of health and safety education, reconstruction, provision of counselling programmes, performance of economic impact studies, learning from mistakes leading to the disaster.

These four actions all work to reduce disaster impact. Strengthening preparedness increases the ability to perform mitigation and recovery activities. Assessment and reflection during the recovery phase should act to strengthen preparedness in the future.

The four main components (mitigation, preparedness, response, and recovery) reduce the impact of disaster for all actors, including tourists, operators, and guides. Ideally, tourist revenues act to strengthen political leadership, but greed-driven leakage acts to reduce it. All components of the disaster management cycle are strengthened by strong political leadership. Also crucial but often absent following disasters is positive feedback from the response to the preparedness component.

Conditions in the mountains are diverse and variable. It is impossible, for example, to see mountain slopes, ridges, and ribs that are identical in incline, length, and relief forms. Alpine walls also differ in incline, length, position, and micro-relief. In the mountains, there are no areas with identical character and locations of cracks, rock ledges, cornices, inner and outer corners, slabs, and so on. Hence, experienced mountaineers and professional guides know how to read the terrain and the meteorological conditions. Precipitation, wind, and severe temperature changes constantly change the situation in the mountains. For example, dry slopes and rocks become dangerous, slippery, or icy after the rain. Strong winds, low temperatures, fogs, thick snow cover, avalanches, and snow eaves, characteristic of mountainous regions, are specific hazards that should be well-known and avoided.

Rapidly advancing storms, thunderstorms, a drop in temperature, or snowfalls (albeit brief) may drastically change the situation. There are cases of warm summer days when clear weather is unexpectedly replaced by a snowstorm. In a few hours, the ridges and slopes of the mountains are covered with a layer of fresh snow 10–15 cm thick, and the temperature drops to 0°C. Such a sharp change in conditions creates a risk of partial or general frostbite and even the death of physically unprepared and poorly equipped travellers. However, difficulties associated with poor weather conditions and difficult mountain topography are not always the main cause of accidents. A well-trained and experienced mountaineer is able to overcome them successfully. With good preparation and an excellent physical condition, rugged terrain and poor weather conditions will be responded to by mobilising, increasing attention, and adopting additional safety measures. Therefore, a mountaineer must be able to foresee and prevent the danger that is ahead, especially in 'easy terrain'. In fact, sometimes, that is more complex than seeing the danger in technically difficult areas. In difficult-to-pass places, the dangers are apparent while in 'easy terrain' they are hidden. It is these hidden and seemingly non-existent dangers that the climber must be able to anticipate in time so that they can take preventive measures.

Mountain tourism has developed in a manner that is not suitable with respect to disaster avoidance. A key driver has been the rapid, opportunistic development of tourist spots and activities to cater to wider audiences at cheaper costs, leading to great tourist pressure. This development has been enabled further by expansions and affordability in transportation networks to improve access and the increased mobility of a growing middle-class population. Pressure in tourism has increased the population of those working in the industry who are exposed to known hazards, often creating a challenge for disaster response in remote areas. Furthermore, a recent study on safety-related behaviour among mountaineers on Mount Kinabalu (4,095 m) concludes that the level of safety-related behaviour on the mountain is moderate. Hence, the local authorities and tourism stakeholders should strengthen safety measures to minimise the risks and potential accidents (Esfahani et al., 2021). Given the great benefit of tourism to national and local economies, governments should look to develop a robust disaster governance approach that balances the need to reduce risks to environmental hazards, while allowing tourism to evolve in a sustainable way that preserves the environment and local cultures but maintains profits (Ziegler et al., 2021).

Notes

1 Flexibility is a property of the human musculoskeletal system that allows for a large amplitude of movement. Great flexibility improves the ability to perform complex bends in a joint or several joints, while avoiding injury.
2 Some routes go beyond the scale adopted here, reaching even 13 (for example, the first ascent of Mission to Mars (WI13) by K. Premrl and T. Emmett in 2020; Slavsky, 2020).
3 Some researchers increase this value to a maximum of 500 m (Luks et al., 2010).

References

Alisow, B. P., Drozdow, O. A., & Rubinsztejn, E. S. (1952). *Kurs klimatologii*. Gidromiet. Izdat.
Allan, N. J. R. (1986). Accessibility and altitudinal zonation models of mountains. *Mountain Research and Development, 6*(3), 185–194. https://doi.org/10.2307/3673384
Allen-Collinson, J. (2018). 'Weather work': Embodiment and weather learning in a national outdoor exercise programme. *Qualitative Research in Sport, Exercise and Health, 10*(1), 63–74. https://doi.org/10.1080/2159676X.2017.1360382
Allen-Collinson, J., Crust, L., & Swann, C. (2018). Embodiment in high-altitude mountaineering: Sensing and working with the weather. *Body & Society, 25*(1), 90–115. https://doi.org/10.1177/1357034X18812947

Apollo, M. (2014). Climbing as a kind of human impact on the high mountain environment – Based on the selected peaks of Seven Summits. *Journal of Selcuk University Natural and Applied Science, 2014*(2), 1061–1071.

Apollo, M. (2017). The true accessibility of mountaineering: The case of the High Himalaya. *Journal of Outdoor Recreation and Tourism, 17,* 29–43. https://doi.org/10.1016/j.jort.2016.12.001

Apollo, M. (2021). *Environmental impacts of mountaineering: A conceptual framework.* Springer. https://doi.org/10.1007/978-3-030-72667-6

Apollo, M., & Andreychouk, V. (2022). *Mountaineering Adventure tourism and local communities: Social, environmental and economic interactions.* Cheltenham: Edward Elgar Publishing.

Attarian, A. (2001). Trends in outdoor adventure education. *Journal of Experiential Education, 24*(3), 141–149. https://doi.org/10.1177/105382590102400304

Bardecki, M., & Wrobel, C. (2015). Protected areas in Nepal: The case for higher entry fees. *Economic Journal of Nepal, 35*(2). https://www.nepjol.info/index.php/EJON/article/view/13418

Barry, R. (2008). *Mountain weather and climate* (3rd ed.). Cambridge University Press.

Beedie, P. (2003). Mountain guiding and adventure tourism: Reflections on the choreography of the experience. *Leisure Studies, 22*(2), 147–167. https://doi.org/10.1080/026143603200068991

Beedie, P., & Hudson, S. (2003). Emergence of mountain-based adventure tourism. *Annals of Tourism Research, 30*(3), 625–643. https://doi.org/10.1016/S0160-7383(03)00043-4

Beniston, M. (2006). Mountain weather and climate: A general overview and a focus on climatic change in the Alps. *Hydrobiologia, 562,* 3–16.

Bhattarai, K., Conway, D., & Shrestha, N. (2005). Tourism, terrorism and turmoil in Nepal. *Annals of Tourism Research, 32*(3), 669–688. https://doi.org/10.1016/j.annals.2004.08.007

Boyes, M., Thompson, S., Grant, B., & Newby, J. (1995). *Risk and responsibility.*

Braun, F., Muhar, A., & Fiebig, M. (2009). Adaptation if the high Alpine trail network to landscape modifications due to climate change – Scenarios for three Austrian mountain regions. *15th International Symposium on Society and Resource Management*, Vienna.

Broadhurst, D., & Smith, C. (2008). *Travel at high altitude.* Medex. http://medex.org.uk/v26%20booklet.pdf

Brymer, E., & Schweitzer, R. (2012). Extreme sports are good for your health: A phenomenological understanding of fear and anxiety in extreme sport. *Journal of Health Psychology, 18*(4), 477–487. https://doi.org/10.1177/1359105312446770

Buckley, R. (1999). An ecological perspective on carrying capacity. *Annals of Tourism Research, 26*(3), 701–703. https://doi.org/10.1016/S0160-7383(99)00013-4

Buckley, R. (2012). Rush as a key motivation in skilled adventure tourism: Resolving the risk recreation paradox. *Tourism Management, 33*(4), 961–970. https://doi.org/10.1016/j.tourman.2011.10.002

Buhalis, D. (2000). Marketing the competitive destination of the future. *Tourism Management, 21*(1), 97–116.

Candela, G., & Figini, P. (2012). *The economics of tourism destinations.* Springer. https://doi.org/http://dx.doi.org/10.1007/978-3-642-20874-4

Chamberlain, K. (1997). *Carrying capacity.*

Clague, J. J., & Stead, D. (2012). *Landslides: Types, mechanisms and modeling.* Cambridge University Press.

Clark, R. N., & Stankey, G. H. (1979). *The recreation opportunity spectrum: A framework for planning, management, and research.* Gen. Tech. Rep. PNW-GTR-098. Portland, OR: U.S. Department of Agriculture, Forest Service, Pacific Northwest Research Station.

CREA Mont Blanc. (2015). *Climate change and its impacts in the Alps.* Research Centre for Alpine Ecosystems. https://creamontblanc.org/en/climate-change-and-its-impacts-alps?utm_content=link2&utm_campaign=articles_id_12453&utm_medium=articles_post&utm_source=ukclimbing

Dahal, R. K., & Hasegawa, S. (2008). Representative rainfall thresholds for landslides in the Nepal Himalaya. *Geomorphology, 100*, 429–443. https://doi.org/10.1016/j.geomorph.2008.01.014

Davis, P. R., Pattinson, K. T. S., Mason, N. P., Richards, P., & Hillebrandt, D. (2005). High altitude illness. *Journal of the Royal Army Medical Corps, 151*(4), 243. https://doi.org/10.1136/jramc-151-04-05

De Freitas, C. (2001). Theory, concepts and methods in tourism climate research. *First International Workshop on Climate, Tourism and Recreation,* Porto Carras, Greece.

De Freitas, C. (2003). Tourism climatology: Evaluating environmental information for decision making and business planning in the recreation and tourism sector. *International Journal of Biometeorology, 48*, 45–54. https://doi.org/10.1007/s00484-003-0177-z

Diener, A. C., & Hagen, J. (2012). *Borders: A very short introduction.* Oxford University Press.

Dwyer, L., & Kim, C. (2003). Destination competitiveness: Determinants and indicators. *Current Issues in Tourism, 6*(5), 369–414. https://doi.org/10.1080/13683500308667962

Elsasser, H., & Bürki, R. (2002). Climate change as a threat to tourism in the Alps. *Climate Research, 20*(3), 253–257. http://www.jstor.org/stable/24866811

Eng, R. C. (2010). *Mountaineering: The Freedom of the Hills.* Mountaineers Books.

Esfahani, M., Khoo, S., Musa, G., Heydari, R., & Keshtidar, M. (2021). The influences of personality and knowledge on safety-related behaviour among climbers. *Current Issues in Tourism,* 1–13. https://doi.org/10.1080/13683500.2021.1873919

Ewert, A. (1985). Why people climb: The relationship of participant motives and experience level to mountaineering. *Journal of Leisure Research, 17*(3), 241–250. https://doi.org/10.1080/00222216.1985.11969634

Ewert, A., & Hollenhorst, S. (1997). Adventure recreation and its implications for wilderness. *3.* International Journal of Wilderness. 3(2), 21–26.

Faullant, R., Matzler, K., & Mooradian, T. A. (2011). Personality, basic emotions, and satisfaction: Primary emotions in the mountaineering experience. *Tourism Management, 32*(6), 1423–1430. https://doi.org/10.1016/j. tourman.2011.01.004

Gallagher, S. A., & Hackett, P. H. (2004). High-altitude illness. *Emergency Medicine Clinics of North America, 22*(2), 329–355, viii. https://doi. org/10.1016/j.emc.2004.02.001

Gundersen, V., Mehmetoglu, M., Inge Vistad, O., & Andersen, O. (2015). Linking visitor motivation with attitude towards management restrictions on use in a national park. *Journal of Outdoor Recreation and Tourism, 9,* 77–86. https://doi.org/10.1016/j.jort.2015.04.004

Haciski, P. (2013). *Jura 2.* Wydawnictwo RING.

Hackett, P. H., & Roach, R. C. (2001). High-altitude illness. *New England Journal of Medicine, 345*(2), 107–114. https://doi.org/10.1056/ nejm200107123450206

Hall, C. M. (2005). Time, space, tourism and social physics. *Tourism Recreation Research,* 30(1), 93–98. http://dx.doi.org/10.1080/02508281.2005. 11081236

Hall, M. (2015). Mountaineering and climate change. In G. Musa, J. Higham, & A. T. Carr (Eds.), *Mountaineering Tourism* (pp. 240–243). Routledge.

Harrison, S. J., Winterbottom, S. J., & Johnson, R. (2005). Changing snow cover and winter tourism and recreation in the Scottish Highlands. In M. Hall & J. Higham (Eds.), *Tourism, recreation and climate change* (pp. 143–154). Channel View.

Hattingh, G. (2000). *The climber's handbook.* New Holland Publishing.

Heather, P. (2013). Glacier retreat and tourism: Insights from New Zealand. *Mountain Research and Development, 33*(4), 463–472. https://doi.org/10.1659/ MRD-JOURNAL-D-12-00073.1

House, S. (2012). *Beyond the mountain.* Patagonia.

Huey, R. B. (2001). The economics of adventure. *The Alpine Journal, 106,* 155–169.

Isserman, M. (2016). *Continental divide: A history of American mountaineering.* W. W. Norton.

Jodłowski, M. (2011). *Zasady dobrej praktyki w zarządzaniu ruchem wspinaczkowym na obszarach chronionych.* Wydawnictwo Uniwersytetu Jagiellońskiego.

Johnson, D. (2004). *The geology of Australia.* Cambridge University Press.

Joyce, K., & Sutton, S. (2009). A method for automatic generation of the Recreation Opportunity Spectrum in New Zealand. *Applied Geography – APPL GEOGR, 29,* 409–418. https://doi.org/10.1016/j.apgeog.2008.11.006

Kaenzig, R., Rebetez, M., & Serquet, G. (2016). Climate change adaptation of the tourism sector in the Bolivian Andes. *Tourism Geographies, 18*(2), 111–128. https://doi.org/10.1080/14616688.2016.1144642

Kamiński, M. (1998). *Moje bieguny. Dzienniki z wypraw 1990–1998.* Ideamedia.

Kiełkowska, M., & Kiełkowski, J. (Eds.). (2003). *Wielka encyklopedia gór i alpinizmu.* Wydawnictwo Stapis.

Kowalewski, Z., & Kurczab, J. (1983). *Na szczytach Himalajów.* Sport i Turystyka.

Kreck, L. A., Guenther, H., & Kopczynski, C. (2000). Saving Mt. Aconcagua. *International Journal of Hospitality & Tourism Administration, 1*(2), 51–64. https://doi.org/10.1300/J149v01n02_03

Lesiecka, A., Szwedo, L., Czapski, B., & Drożdż, T. (2012, 29 September 2012). *Lęk i wolność* III Konferencja Medycyny Górskiej, Medical University of Silesia.

Lindberg, K., McCool, S., & Stankey, G. (1997). Rethinking carrying capacity. *Annals of Tourism Research, 24*(2), 461–465. https://doi.org/10.1016/S0160-7383(97)80018-7

Lischke, V., Byhahn, C., Westphal, K., & Kessler, P. (2001). Mountaineering accidents in the European Alps: Have the numbers increased in recent years? *Wilderness & Environmental Medicine, 12*(2), 74–80. https://doi.org/10.1580/1080-6032(2001)012[0074:maitea]2.0.co;2

Luks, A. M., McIntosh, S. E., Grissom, C. K., Auerbach, P. S., Rodway, G. W., Schoene, R. B., Zafren, K., & Hackett, P. H. (2010). Wilderness Medical Society consensus guidelines for the prevention and treatment of acute altitude illness. *Wilderness & Environmental Medicine, 21*(2), 146–155. https://doi.org/10.1016/j.wem.2010.03.002

Luks, A. M., McIntosh, S. E., Grissom, C. K., Auerbach, P. S., Rodway, G. W., Schoene, R. B., Zafren, K., & Hackett, P. H. (2014). Wilderness Medical Society practice guidelines for the prevention and treatment of acute altitude illness: 2014 update. *Wilderness & Environmental Medicine, 25*(4 Suppl), S4–14. https://doi.org/10.1016/j.wem.2014.06.017

Makowski, J. (2006). *Geografia fizyczna świata.* Polskie Wydawnictwo Naukowe.

Marek, A., & Wieczorek, M. (2015). Tourist traffic in the Aconcagua massif area. *Quaestiones Geographicae, 34*(3), 65–76. http://geoinfo.amu.edu.pl/qg/archives/2015/QG343_065-076.pdf

Maurer, E. (2009). Cold war, 'thaw' and 'everlasting friendship': Soviet mountaineers and Mount Everest, 1953–1960. *The International Journal of the History of Sport, 26*(4), 484–500. https://doi.org/10.1515/quageo-2015-0022

Mayor, A. (2021). *Who were the first recreational mountain climbers?* Retrieved 27/03/2021 from https://www.wondersandmarvels.com/2013/06/who-were-the-first-recreational-mountain-climbers.html

Messerli, B., & Ives, J. (1997). *Mountains of the world: A global priority.* Parthenon Publishing.

Middleton, V. T. C. (1994). *Marketing in travel and tourism.* Butterworth Heinemann.

Middleton, V. T. C., Fyall, A., Morgan, M., & Ranchhod, A. (2009). *Marketing in Travel and Tourism.* Butterworth-Heinemann.

Middleton, V. T., & Hawkins, R. (1998). *Sustainable tourism: A marketing perspective.* Butterworth Heinemann.

Montesquieu, C. L. (1777). *The spirit of laws* (Vol. 1). T. Evans. https://oll. libertyfund.org/title/montesquieu-complete-works-vol-1-the-spirit-of-laws

Morrison, C., & Pickering, C. M. (2013). Perceptions of climate change impacts, adaptation and limits to adaption in the Australian Alps: The ski-tourism industry and key stakeholders. *Journal of Sustainable Tourism, 21*(2), 173–191. https://doi.org/10.1080/09669582.2012.681789

Mourey, J., Marcuzzi, M., Ravanel, L., & Pallandre, F. (2019). Effects of climate change on high Alpine mountain environments: Evolution of mountaineering routes in the Mont Blanc massif (Western Alps) over half a century. *Arctic, Antarctic, and Alpine Research, 51*(1), 176–189. https://doi. org/10.1080/15230430.2019.1612216

Munteanu, A. (2010). Conceptualizing and composing tourism accessibility. *Lucrările Seminarului Geografic "dimitrie Cantemir", 30,* 125–133.

Musa, G., & Thirumoorthi, T. (2015). Health and safety issues in mountaineering tourism. In G. Musa, J. Higham, & A. T. Carr (Eds.), *Mountaineering tourism* (pp. 294–312). Routledge.

Nepal, S. K. (2000). Tourism in protected areas: The Nepalese Himalaya. *Annals of Tourism Research, 27*(3), 661–681. https://doi.org/10.1016/ S0160-7383(99)00105-X

Nepal, S. K. (2008). Tourism-induced rural energy consumption in the Annapurna region of Nepal. *Tourism Management, 29*(1), 89–100. https://doi. org/10.1016/j.tourman.2007.03.024

Nepal, S. K., & Mu, Y. (2015). Mountaineering, commodification and risk perceptions in Nepal's Mt Everest Region. In G. Musa, J. Higham, & A. T. Carr (Eds.), *Mountaineering tourism* (pp. 250–264). Routledge.

Noetzli, J., Hoelzle, M., & Haeberli, W. (2003, 01/01). Mountain permafrost and recent Alpine rockfall events: A GIS-based approach to determine critical factors. *Eighth International Conference on Permafrost, Lisse, Netherlands.*

Nunes, P., Cai, M., Ferrise, R., Moriondo, M., & Bindi, M. (2013). An econometric analysis of climate change impacts on tourism flows: An empirical evidence from the region of Tuscany, Italy. *International Journal of Ecological Economics and Statistics, 31,* 1–20.

Nyaupane, G. P. (2015). Mountaineering on Mt Everest: Evolution, economy, ecology and ethics. In G. Musa, J. Higham, & A. T. Carr (Eds.), *Mountaineering tourism.* Routledge.

Outdoor Foundation (2016). Outdoor Participation Report 2016. Retrieved 10/5/2016 from www.outdoorfoundation.org/pdf/ResearchParticipation 2016Topline.pdf

Paryski, H.W. (1951). Tatry Wysokie. Tom 1. Sport i Turystyka.

Paryski, H.W. (1976). Tatry Wysokie. Tom 20. Sport i Turystyka.

Perry, A. H., & Smith, K. (1996). Recreation and tourism. In *Department of the environment, climate change report.* London.

Pomfret, G. (2006). Mountaineering adventure tourists: A conceptual framework for research. *Tourism Management, 27*(1), 113–123. https://doi. org/10.1016/j.tourman.2004.08.003

Price, M. F., & Steiner, A. (2004). *Conservation and sustainable development in mountain areas.* https://portals.iucn.org/library/node/8533

Prideaux, B. (2000). The resort development spectrum – A new approach to modeling resort development. *Tourism Management, 21*(3), 225–240. https://doi.org/10.1016/S0261-5177(99)00055-2

Pröbstl-Haider, U., Dabrowska, K., & Haider, W. (2016). Risk perception and preferences of mountain tourists in light of glacial retreat and permafrost degradation in the Austrian Alps. *Journal of Outdoor Recreation and Tourism, 13*, 66–78. https://doi.org/10.1016/j.jort.2016.02.002

Prohaska, F. (1970). Distinctive bioclimatic parameters of the subtropical-tropical Andes. *International Journal of Biometeorology, 14*(1), 1–12. https://doi.org/10.1007/BF01440674

Pugh, L. G. (1962). Physiological and medical aspects of the Himalayan scientific and mountaineering expedition, 1960–61. *British Medical Journal, 2*(5305), 621–627. https://doi.org/10.1136/bmj.2.5305.621

Purdie, H., Gomez, C., & Espiner, S. (2015). Glacier recession and the changing rockfall hazard: Implications for glacier tourism [https://doi.org/10.1111/nzg.12091]. *New Zealand Geographer, 71*(3), 189–202. https://doi.org/10.1111/nzg.12091

Radwańska-Paryska, Z and Paryski, H.W. (1995). *Wielka Encyklopedia Tatrzańska.* Wyd. Górskie.

Reiter, R., & Munzert, K. (1982). Values of UV- and global radiation in the northern Alps. *Archives for Meteorology, Geophysics, and Bioclimatology, Series B, 30*(3), 239–246. https://doi.org/10.1007/BF02323363

Richardson, R. B., & Loomis, J. (2004). Adaptive recreation planning and climate change: A contingent visitation approach. *Ecological Economics, 50*(1–2), 83–99. https://EconPapers.repec.org/RePEc:eee:ecolec:v:50:y:2004:i:1-2:p:83-99

Ring, T., Salkin, R. M., & La Boda, S. (1994). *International dictionary of historic places.* Fitzroy Dearborn Publishers.

Ritter, F., Fiebig, M., & Muhar, A. (2012). Impacts of global warming on mountaineering: A classification of phenomena affecting the Alpine Trail Network. *Mountain Research and Development, 32*(1), 4–15. https://doi.org/10.1659/MRD-JOURNAL-D-11-00036.1

Ryn, Z. (1967). Zaburzenia psychiczne w chorobie gorskiej wysokosciowej. *Psychiatria Polska, 3*, 331–335.

Ryn, Z. (1988). Psychopathology in mountaineering-mental disturbances under high-altitude stress. *International Journal of Sports Medicine, 9*(2), 163–169. https://doi.org/10.1055/s-2007-1024998

Ryn, Z. (2016). *Góry. Medycyna Antropologia.* Medycyna Praktyczna.

Salkeld, A., & Bonington, C. (1998). *World mountaineering.* Mitchell Beazley.

Sauberer, F., & Dirmhirn, I. (1965). Das Strahlungsklima. In F. Steinhauser, O. Eckel, & F. Lauscher (Eds.), *Klimatographie von Österreich* (pp. 13–102). Österreichische Akademie der Wissenschaften.

Savage, D. A., & Torgler, B. (2015). *The times they are a changin': The effect of institutional change on cooperative behaviour at 26,000 ft over sixty years.* Palgrave Macmillan. https://doi.org/10.1057/9781137525154

Schöffl, V., Morrison, A., Hefti, U., Ullrich, S., & Küpper, T. (2011). The UIAA medical commission injury classification for mountaineering and climbing sports. *Wilderness & Environmental Medicine, 22*(1), 46–51. https://doi.org/10.1016/j.wem.2010.11.008

Schussman, L. C., Lutz, L. J., Shaw, R. R., & Bohnn, C. R. (1990). The epidemiology of mountaineering and rock climbing accidents. *Journal of Wilderness Medicine, 1*(4), 235–248. https://doi.org/10.1580/0953-9859-1.4.235

Scott, D. (2006). Climate change and sustainable tourism in the 21st century. In *Tourism research: Policy, planning, and prospects.* (pp. 175–248). Departamento de Geografa, Universidad de Waterloo.

Scott, D., Jones, B., & Konopek, J. (2007). Implications of climate and environmental change for nature-based tourism in the Canadian Rocky Mountains: A case study of Waterton Lakes National Park. *Tourism Management, 28*(2), 570–579. https://doi.org/10.1016/j.tourman.2006.04.020

Simpson, J. (1988). *Touching the void.* Jonathan Cape.

Slavsky, B. (2020). Mission to Mars (WI13)—The hardest ice climb in the world. *Climbing Magazine* (Online). Retrieved 20/42021 from https://www.climbing.com/news/video-mission-to-mars-wi13-the-hardest-ice-climb-in-the-world/

Soles, C., & Powers, P. (2003). *Climbing: Expedition planning.* Mountaineers Books.

Stewart, A. (2012). *Kilimanjaro – A complete trekker's guide: Preparations, practicalities and trekking routes to the 'Roof of Africa'.* Cicerone Press Ltd.

Szymczak, R. (2009a). *Poradnik dla podróżnika wysokogórskiego.* MEDEverest. http://medeverest.com/publikacje.html

Szymczak, R. (2009b). *Wpływ przewlekłej hipoksji wysokogórskiej na wybrane parametry życiowe organizmu człowieka.* Uniwersytet Gdański. Gdańsk.

Timothy, D. J. (2002). Tourism in borderlands: Competition, complementarity, and crossfrontier cooperation. In S. Krakover & Y. Gradus (Eds.), *Tourism in frontier areas* (pp. 233–258). Lexington Books.

Trayers, F. J. (2004). Wilderness preventive medicine. *Wilderness & Environmental Medicine, 15*(1), 1–3. https://doi.org/10.1580/1080-6032(2004)015[0001:wpm]2.0.co;2

Trepińska, J. (2002). *Górskie klimaty.* Instytut Geografii i Gospodarki Przestrzennej Uniwersytetu Jagiellońskiego.

Vardy, J., Vardy, J., & Judge, K. (2006). Acute mountain sickness and ascent rates in trekkers above 2500 m in the Nepali Himalaya. *Aviation, Space, and Environmental Medicine, 77*(7), 742–744.

von Rohrscheidt, A. M. (2010). *Regionalne szlaki tematyczne. Idea, potencjał, organizacja.* Proksenia.

Wahl, E. W. (1953). Singularities and the general circulation. *Journal of Atmospheric Sciences, 10*(1), 42–45. https://doi.org/10.1175/1520-0469(1953)010<0042:SATGC>2.0.CO;2

Ward, M. (1975). *Mountain medicine.* Crosby Lockwood Staples.

Weil, J. V. (2004). Sleep at high altitude. *High Altitude Medicine & Biology, 5*(2), 180–189. https://doi.org/10.1089/1527029041352162

West, J., Schoene, R., Luks, A., & Milledge, J. (2012). *High altitude medicine and physiology* (5th ed.). CRC Press.

Williams, E. S., Taggart, P., & Carruthers, M. (1978). Rock climbing: Observations on heart rate and plasma catecholamine concentrations and the influence of oxprenolol. *British Journal of Sports Medicine, 12*(3), 125–128. https://doi.org/10.1136/bjsm.12.3.125

Wilson, M. H., Newman, S., & Imray, C. H. (2009). The cerebral effects of ascent to high altitudes. *Lancet Neurology, 8*(2), 175–191. https://doi.org/10.1016/s1474-4422(09)70014-6

Wyss-Dunant, E. (1953). Acclimatisation. In M. Kurz (Ed.), *The mountain world* (pp. 110–117). George Allen & Unwin Ltd.

Xiao, X., Manning, R., Lawson, S., Valliere, W., & Krymkowski, D. (2018). Indicators for a transportation recreation opportunity spectrum in national parks. *Journal of Park and Recreation Administration, 36*(1), 90–112. https://doi.org/10.18666/JPRA-2018-V36-I1-8117

Ziegler, A. D., Wasson, R. J., Sundriya, Y., Srivastava, P., Sasges, G., Ramchunder, S. J., Nepal, S. K., McAdoo, B. G., Gillen, J., Bishwokarma, D., Bhardwaj, A., & Apollo, M. (2021). A call for reducing tourism risk to environmental hazards in the Himalaya. *Environmental Hazards [under review].*

Zurick, D. N. (1992). Adventure Travel and sustainable tourism in the peripheral economy of Nepal. *Annals of the Association of American Geographers, 82*(4), 608–628. https://doi.org/10.1111/j.1467-8306.1992.tb01720.x

3 Tourism experiences and behaviours in mountain areas

Abstract

This chapter outlines the types of tourists who visit mountain areas. It provides an overview of their common behavioural patterns and discusses the implications of these behaviours. It then considers the personal impacts of mountaineering and the 'transformational experiences' it may cause. It provides evidence that some participants are motivated to engage in mountaineering tourism because of 'critical incidents' in their lives. The chapter concludes with a discussion on ethical issues related to mountaineering activity.

3.1 Evolution of mountaineers

In general, the tens of millions of tourists who travel to mountains for hiking, trekking, and mountain climbing represent two main groups of people: (1) those who want to experience an adventure and (2) pilgrims. Adventure tourists are involved in all mountaineering activities, while pilgrims guided by spiritual motivations mainly hike or trek to holy places in the mountains. However, these two groups have entirely different motivations (secular or sacred), and hence their mountain journeys are different and require different management strategies. Furthermore, mountaineers participating in high-altitude mountaineering tourism for adventure purposes can also be divided into two groups: (1) those who organise their expedition themselves (without a guide) and (2) those who rely on the help of service companies and guides. These two groups of people also therefore have different motivations, and they aim to satisfy different needs, which can be characterised by the needs pyramid created by Maslow (1954). The development of extreme sports has given rise to people heading

DOI: 10.4324/9781003095323-3

Figure 3.1 Maslow's model – hierarchy of human needs (redrawn from Maslow, 1954).

to mountains in search of new, often strong emotions and sensations. It is quite difficult (if not impossible) to specify reasons why people become interested in high mountains. Generally, the motives of the two main groups of people who visit high mountains today are, according to Maslow's (1954) hierarchy of needs, self-actualisation (self-sufficient climbers) and esteem (climbers using the services of paid guides; Figure 3.1). What is more, at the 'lower' level of esteem is the need for respect from others, and this may include the need for status, recognition, fame, prestige, and attention. The need for respect is a perfect fit for mountaineering participants taking part in organised (commercial) mountain expeditions. They may be looking for respect (recognition) in the eyes of others and a positive image as seen by others. Unfortunately, more and more often, independent mountaineers, guided by specific rules, are being replaced, as the Polish climber Piotr Morawski accurately described it, by tourists with overgrown ambition (Nowacki, 2009).

The case of British mountaineer David Sharp, who in 2006 died under a rock overhang known by climbers as 'Green Boots' Cave' (named after a climber wearing green boots whose body remains there), is a

Table 3.1 The number of climbers above base camp on Everest between 1950–1989 and 1990–2009 and the dynamics of changes

Routes	Number of climbers above base camp in a selected period		The dynamics of growth rates in the number of climbers between 1950–1989 and 1990–2009 (%)
	1950–1989	1990–2009	
Non-commercial	1,307	1,253	−4.31
Commercial	829	5,742	692.64

Source: completed by the author based on data from Salisbury and Hawley, 2011.

perfect illustration of this phenomenon. His death caused a great stir in the climbing community as Sharp had been passed by 30–40 mountaineers being guided by commercial enterprises heading for the summit who did not attempt to rescue him while he sat with arms clasped around his legs, dying (e.g. see Heinrichs 2010).

Globalisation and related commercialisation can be seen at every level of mountaineering – from trekking to climbing. Even on the highest peaks, such as Everest, commercialised routes are the most frequented (Table 3.1). Today, commercialism introduces to the mountain environment people who have inadequate and excessive expectations of accommodation, transport, and food (especially their quality). In one example, the demand for a barbecue at the main base near Aconcagua (Plaza de Mulas, 4,350 m) led to its provision, but, unfortunately, some participants found the quality of the meat below their expectations. Due to the globalisation of this sport, its counterculture, which was once directed against modernity and the bourgeoisie, is completely disappearing (Okupnik, 2002). This phenomenon, although referring mainly to mountaineering, is relevant to all high-mountain-climbing tourism and especially to the so-called commercial partner expeditions (Wengel & Apollo, 2021). In themselves, these are a positive development: more experienced colleagues take those with less experience on an expedition. A problem arises when distinctions become 'foggy' and vague and commercial companies are used. Wengel and Apollo (2021) describe several cases leading to dangerous situations, sometimes ending in the death of the participant or participants.

The motivations of mountaineers are of great importance because those who love mountains care more about them. Currently, high-altitude-climbing (adventure) tourism, which was once an elite phenomenon, has become a mass activity. Unfortunately, the increase in the number of participants and the change in the participants' profiles means that the negative environmental impact on the fragile high-altitude mountain environment will be more significant and apparent. All this is further combined with the commercialisation and commodification of high-mountain-climbing tourism. For example, when the Marangu Route (the most popular route to Kilimanjaro) became available to the public, its capacity was estimated at 15,000 people per year (Apollo, 2010). This value was exceeded in the same year. In 2015, it was exceeded by almost 4 times. The desire for profit wins.

People travelling to or near high mountains for religious reasons have completely different motivations. The motive for undertaking the effort required for a pilgrimage may be the desire to make amends for wrongs committed or to express a petition to a deity, such as for health or well-being (e.g. see Barber. 1993). Making pilgrimages to holy places is very common in many religions. Pilgrims visit – depending on their religion – temples or holy places, such as peaks, lakes, and rivers. Pilgrimages to temples located in mountainous regions are the oldest form of tourism, practised since time immemorial. The Greeks paid homage to the gods on Mount Olympus, as did the Maasai on Kilimanjaro and the Incas on the Andean peaks (Gawlik et al., 2021; Shinde & Olsen, 2020). Currently, some of the most famous mountain regions visited for religious reasons include Kailash in China, the Kii mountains and Mount Fuji in Japan, Mount Sinai in Egypt, Coropuna and Ausangate in Peru, and the Llullaillaco volcano in Argentina, among others. There are many temples in the Himalayas, such as the Badrinath Temple (India), which in 2011 alone was visited by nearly 1 million (980,667) believers (DoT, 2012).

The behaviour of pilgrims in mountain environments differs among representatives of different religions. For example, Christians from Europe and Buddhists from Japan have a completely different approach to the environment compared to Hindus. This is due to cultural differences and has nothing to do with the type of religion because in each of them, the natural environment – as the work of the Creator – is sacred (Apollo, 2016; Apollo et al., 2020; Shinde & Olsen, 2020; Taylor, 2007; Watling, 2009). Unfortunately, not all pilgrims take this seriously. Undoubtedly, sacred Hindu sites are among the most polluted in the world (Alley, 1998; Apollo et al., 2020; Sati, 2014, 2015; Timothy & Nyaupane, 2009).

Mountain regions famous for their majestic scenery and surrounded by an aura of sanctity are becoming more and more desirable tourist destinations for people looking for both the sacred and the profane (see Sati, 2015). High-altitude-climbing tourism – whether motivated by the need to experience an adventure or the desire to go on a pilgrimage – takes the form of a mass movement. In some cases, the traditional understanding of mountaineering and how one should behave in the mountain environment is lost. Others disregard the will of the Creator (displaying a lack of respect for nature), and, to a large extent, these affect the natural mountain environment that is susceptible to changes and the human communities inhabiting it.

3.2 Types of mountaineering tourists

Historically, since its popularisation in the 20th century, mountaineering was a venture for the elite, such as professional mountaineers and athletes. However, with the commodification of tourism and the increasing demand for adventure tourism, mountaineering has become a commodity for regular tourists (Johnston & Edwards, 1994; Marek & Wieczorek, 2015; Nepal, 2000; Pomfret, 2006; Zurick, 1992). This has resulted in a growing number of inexperienced and less-skilled adventurers aiming to scale a summit with no previous experience in mountaineering and climbing; this is also seen even on the world's top peak, Everest (Elmes & Barry, 1999; Messerli & Ives, 1997; Mu et al., 2019).

According to Salisbury and Hawley (2011), between 1990 and 2009, almost 54 per cent of all climbers above the base camp on Ama Dablam (6,812 m), Cho You (8,188 m), and Everest (8,848 m) were on the commercial routes (the most accessible routes used by commercial groups and supported by a large number of expedition support staff). In the case of Everest, when comparing periods before and after 1990, the percentage of climbers opting for non-commercial routes declined by 4.3 per cent, and, at the same time, the percentage of mountaineers on commercial routes increased by almost 700 per cent (Apollo, 2017). Furthermore, existing studies clearly show the differences between inexperienced and experienced climbers (Ewert, 1985; Houge Mackenzie & Kerr, 2012; Pomfret, 2012). Ewert (1985) suggests that the higher the experience level, the higher the tendency to adhere to core-related motivations such as thrill, personal challenge, and locus of control. Similarly, an inexperienced climber is more motivated by factors such as recognition and socialising. Pomfret (2011) highlights that especially inexperienced mountaineers who travel on commercially guided expeditions are subject to reduced risk levels. Houge Mackenzie and Kerr (2012) note that inexperienced mountain tourists aspiring to a successful adventure tourism experience rely on guiding companies.

Researchers emphasise that inexperienced climbers are attracted to mountains not only as mountains become more accessible (Apollo, 2017) but also due to the popularity of 'bucket lists' (a list of epic experiences and must-visit places to be achieved before death

(Thurnell-Read, 2017); initiatives like 'peak-bagging' – an attempt to reach a collection of summits (Apollo et al., 2021); and challenges like the Seven Summits – with the aim to reach the highest mountain on each continent (Bass et al., 1986). Research shows that more inexperienced people attempt to undertake mountaineering on so-called non-technical high-altitude peaks like Kilimanjaro (5,895 m; Andrew et al., 2009) and Aconcagua (6,962 m; Borm et al., 2011). However, research indicates that even at the lower ranges of high altitude (above 2,500 m), mountaineers are at greater risk and danger (Ewert, 1994) and likely to even succumb to altitude sickness (Musa et al., 2004).

Based on the research of Wengel and Apollo (2021), as well as participation in expeditions (Apollo, 2013), mountaineering experience, and observation of other climbers and mountaineers during fieldwork, we identify three distinct categories of contemporary mountaineers: true mountaineers, recreational mountaineers, and novice mountaineers.

True mountaineers are climbers who are interested in exploring challenging and off-the-beaten-track mountain destinations. True mountaineers have similar technical mountaineering skill levels to elite and professional mountaineers, but they rarely guide expeditions for commercial purposes. Instead, they are leaders of small teams of friends, colleagues, or members of alpine clubs. True mountaineers can independently plan expeditions and are familiar with using auxiliary means for climbing (crampons, ropes, carabiners, ice axes, etc.).

Furthermore, they are familiar with the environment, terrain patterns, and weather conditions; they know how to use maps, modern GPS, and satellite equipment. Hence, they are well-prepared for emergencies and can deal with potentially life-threatening challenges. In terms of expedition organisation, true mountaineers operate independently and seldom rely on the help of commercial guiding companies. Our findings show that this type of mountaineering tourist may contract a guiding company only to assist with necessary issues such as obtaining climbing permits and organising logistics to the base camp. True mountaineers plan their expeditions well in advance and usually spend a long time at the mountain destination.

The second category of contemporary mountaineering tourists is called *recreational mountaineers*. They are semi-professional mountaineers who occasionally climb in high-altitude environments for recreational purposes. Similarly to true mountaineers, recreational mountaineers are driven to explore remote mountain destinations. They have good technical mountaineering skills, and they are eager to improve their skills; often, they do so by improving their experience through progress from more accessible to more challenging expeditions. Recreational mountaineers have experience in expedition preparation (but usually, their experience is not enough to lead a group of fellow climbers). They know how to use auxiliary means for climbing (crampons, ropes, carabiners, ice axes, etc.) and can navigate and survive in a high-altitude environment. As with true mountaineers, they are well prepared for challenging and emergency situations. Recreational mountaineers often travel on non-commercial independent expeditions organised by mountaineering clubs or their more experienced peers.

Novice mountaineers form the last group of mountaineers that emerged from our research findings. Often novice mountaineers visit high-altitude mountain environments just once to experience the 'adventure of a lifetime'. Novice mountaineers are least experienced in terms of technical mountaineering skill levels (and often they have never engaged in mountaineering or climbing) but have a good fitness level to engage in adventure activities. Many novice mountaineers lack a basic understanding of the environment, maps, and weather, and often they have no experience in using mountaineering tools. On some expeditions, learning basic mountaineering skills is part of the expedition programme. Novice mountaineers therefore rely solely on (commercial) expedition companies, guides, and porters. Novice mountaineers represent the largest group of modern mountaineers, and they create an increasingly growing demand for the commodified mountaineering adventure. They usually buy packaged mountain trips to the most popular and easily assessable novice peaks. In our experience, novice mountaineers are the least prepared for emergencies and often rely on emergency evacuation by helicopter. Our experience and observation show that novice mountaineers have limited time to travel and follow (often too-short) schedules for expeditions. Short timeframes for expeditions (often without any reserve days for bad weather conditions or emergencies) frequently result in emergency evacuation (e.g. due to acute mountain sickness or a lack of technical skills or physical strength to maintain speedy ascents scheduled by expedition companies).

3.3 Personal impacts of mountaineering

This section discusses the personal impacts of mountaineering and how people who have experienced 'critical incidents' in their lives (Casalis, 2006; Moore, 2017) embark on transformational journeys through mountaineering tourism. Casalis (2006) defines a critical incident as 'an event out of the range of normal experience – one which is sudden and unexpected, makes you lose control, involves the perception of a threat to life and can include elements of physical or emotional loss' (p. 9). Some of the mountaineers we met during our time in the mountains recalled negative critical incidents such as illness, car accidents, divorce, or loss of a friend or family member. However, although a critical incident refers to an outstanding event that impacts a person's life, it is not necessarily a dramatic or negative event (Moore, 2017). Some of the positive critical incident events from mountaineers included graduation from university, feeling empowered, meeting new friends, watching films, or reading books, which impacted the person and motivated them to engage in mountaineering. Critical incidents are 'emotionally charged' turning points in one's worldview (Fook et al., 2000; Tripp, 2011), which encourage an individual to 'stop and think' (Stepney, 2006, p. 1032).

Lester (2004) argues that mountaineering activity may be attractive mainly to divided selves who seek a sense of freedom and a sense of power, energy, and vitality. Some mountaineers recalled how they grew personally by participating in mountaineering, especially if they started as novice and inexperienced mountaineers or novice mountaineers and further progressed to become recreational mountaineers (Wengel & Apollo, 2021).

The motives related to the self for participation in mountaineering, such as seeking contact with a better self, assertion or conquest of self, or escape from self, aim to enhance a sense of integration and diminish the sense of fragmentation (Lester, 2004). In some cases, during expeditions, participants shared that their mountaineering experiences had led to the significant alteration and transformation of their worldviews, sometimes resulting in a change of occupation and life direction.

Recently, scholars have recognised and acknowledged the transformational potential of tourism (Reisinger, 2013). According to Kottler (1998), a transformational tourism experience is driven by 'intellectual curiosity, emotional need, or physical challenge' (p. 26). Willig (2008) emphasises that as a form of transformational tourism, extreme sports provide physical challenge, therapeutic experience, psychological balance and facilitate 'opportunities to test, play with, and possibly transcend the confines of the self' (p. 700). Furthermore, Brymer (2013) challenges the hedonistic risk-focused perspective on extreme sports and highlights the transformative nature of extreme adventures in terms of self-awareness, the ability to see others more positively and openly, and our connection to the natural world.

As a form of adventure and transformational tourism, mountaineering tourism combines physicality with self-development by using mountaineering challenges as the vehicle for self-discovery and improvement. Immersion in a different environment through mountaineering activity removes people from the everyday, familiar, and habitual environments. In terms of the personal impacts of mountaineering, participants report exploring and mastering

- mental resilience and endurance,
- stress and fear,
- courage and confidence,
- immersion in 'flow' (Csikszentmihalyi, 2014).

When participating in mountaineering activity, mountaineers challenge themselves physically and mentally while surrounded by nature and mountains. Harper and Webster (2017) emphasise that high-altitude environments, cultural immersion, or other challenging situations can facilitate growth and development. Externally, mountaineering tourists could use the tourist experience for a physical challenge; however, mountaineering tourism is often a journey of self-discovery. Hence, we argue that as a form of immersive learning and transformational tourism, mountaineering impacts the personality and allows us to learn about self, life, and the world around us and enhance our ability to adapt and grow.

3.4 Ethics and mountaineering

For the past two decades, adventure tourism has been growing, and quantitative (e.g. the number of participants) as well as qualitative changes (e.g. the appearance of mass tourists) in mountaineering affect the broadly understood high-mountain environment. In order to limit negative impacts and foster stable and responsible development of the reception environment, for decades there have been specific rules that should be followed by all entities participating in tourism – central and regional administration, local communities, organising units (tourism industry), as well as and, maybe most importantly, the tourists themselves. Such rules (e.g. ethical guidelines and codes of conduct) were contained in the Global Code of Ethics for Tourism (GKET), which was adopted on 30 October 1999, by the General Assembly of the World Tourism Organization (WTO), Resolution A/RES/406 (XIII) (UNWTO, 1999). The GKET also addresses a range of trade, security, and humanitarian phenomena that impact tourism in a variety of ways.

The Code is a specific set of fundamental norms and customs generally accepted in tourism. Its use in qualified tourism must be appropriately adapted. For each qualification, the code should be extended with specific standards resulting from the conditions of tourism activity (the form of qualified tourism, the degree of specialisation, or the reception environment's characteristics.) Standards and customs in mountaineering should be considered based on three aspects:

- Internal social norms – the responsibility for one's own safety and that of the partner(s), and the readiness to help other tourist traffic participants in danger. In high-mountain regions, the application of these standards may turn out to be unfeasible – it is not possible to take care of another person who has exceeded the limits of their physical abilities (see Section 2.6), when you have exceeded your own. A clear example of this is the controversial death of David Sharp at the 'Green Boots' Cave' (see Section 3.2). Leaving a team member is the worst offence against mountaineering ethics (Eng, 2010; Klemensiewicz, 1937), albeit a very controversial one.
- External social and social norms – the tourist's impact on the reception environment (natural and social). They touch upon the consequences of failure to respect nature and the society that inhabits it. Sloppy and thoughtless behaviour in this respect leads to irreversible environmental changes, both natural and human. As many tourists come from developed countries and many of the recipient/host countries are developing countries, inhabitants of mountain areas are most exposed to these changes (sociocultural and natural; Apollo, 2015; Apollo & Andreychouk, 2022). This is all the more so because – as numerous studies show – tourists behave differently than usual when on holiday (Przecławski, 1997). Many tourists not only do not respect the local population's social and cultural values but also treat the trip as an exemption from the obligation to observe moral and social norms prevailing in their own living environment. Responsible development in this area is ensured by various non-profit organisations, including the Leave No Trace Center for Outdoor Ethics, founded in 1994, promoting a set of rules and standards of conduct to minimise the impact on the environment, or, in other words, 'Leave No Trace' behaviour.
- Passage cleanliness standards – rules about the goal and how to achieve it. It is forbidden to operate on peaks that are temporarily or permanently excluded, for example those that are protected

due to nature or the beliefs of indigenous peoples. Also, mountaineers are not allowed to use inappropriate climbing equipment (e.g. invasive) on paths that prohibit this equipment. It is considered highly unethical to overestimate the difficulties of a path or passage. It is also amoral to describe (tell) exploits beyond their actual value. Some excessively exaggerate their achievement while talking to non-specialists in the field of high-mountain tourism or listeners who are inexperienced in mountaineering. This would not go unnoticed in the eyes of professional mountaineers and industry specialists.

Unlike other adventure sports, mountaineering does not have many formal rules, regulations, and governance schemes, but mountaineers adhere to philosophies, ethics, and techniques (which may vary by continent or mountaineering period; Kublak, 2014). For as long as mountaineering has existed, mountaineers have tried to maintain a specific set of ethical rules and standards. However, these ethical principles have never been officially formalised, but instead, passed on from experienced mountaineers to novices (Hoibian, 2016).

Historically, mountaineers have sought a balance between challenge, safety, and climbing techniques used in various regions. More recently, the mountaineering community has voiced concerns about the impact on host cultures and the environment. The ethics of mountaineering include specific moral behaviours underpinning climbing activity in various environments, both natural and human (Eng, 2010; Kiełkowska & Kiełkowski, 2003).

We would like to draw attention to two codes of ethics for mountaineering. The first set of guidelines is called The Code of High Mountain Tourism. This code was written in 1937 by a Polish physicist and physical chemist who was also an accomplished mountaineer. *The Decalogue* of Klemensiewicz (1937, pp. 118–119) presents a set of norms and customs for mountaineers:

- Protect the nature of high mountains, rocks, plants, animals. Do not make noise or litter in the mountains; try to stay out of sight as much as possible.
- Respect the distinct customs of the mountain people and their property. Treat them humanely and honestly, but without being overly generous.
- Use mountain facilities (paths and shelters) according to their purpose and nature and help maintain them. Understand that in high regions everything is more expensive.

- Be polite to other tourists, but do not impose yourself. Behave in such a way that your presence is not a burden to anyone.
- When bound by rope with others, be kind, sacrificial, loyal, and compatible.
- Help your neighbour in times of need; you may need help at some point too.
- Do not engage in things that overwhelm you and your companions and do not persuade them to act unwisely.
- Try to stay fit so that you can fulfil your duties as a team member and not be a burden on others. If you feel unwell, descend to a lower altitude.
- Prepare for each trip carefully and conduct it carefully, remembering that you have responsibilities towards your family and society.
- Don't try to impress laymen with stories about your accomplishments or you will lose the respect of those you should care about.

The second, contemporary set of guidelines was released by the International Mountaineering and Climbing Federation at the General Assembly of the Union Internationale des Associations d'Alpinisme (UIAA) in Porto, Portugal, in October 2009 and is called the UIAA Mountain Ethics Declaration. The UIAA Mountain Ethics Declaration draws on the previous ethical standards, including the Mountain Code, the Summit Charter, and the Tirol Declaration.

The UIAA Mountain Ethics Declaration concerns mountaineers' behaviours, attitudes, and responsibilities to themselves, each other, the natural environment, and the culture and traditions of host countries (UIAA, 2009). The Declaration considers access to mountains and natural environments a fundamental human right if done in a responsible manner.

Ever since mountaineering became a sport, climbers have had to balance exposure to danger with the proper margin of safety. At the dawn of mountaineering, the goal was simple – to reach the top; climbers chose the most straightforward route, often carrying ladders, anchoring devices, and other equipment used in storming medieval castles. However, after the highest mountains of the Alps were conquered, climbers began to look for more challenging routes to their peaks. Albert F. Mummery, an Englishman, said the rules of the game should be based on what he called 'fair opportunity'; he climbed without professional guides and gave up hooks and ladders. Mummery became one of the best climbers of his time and raised the bar of the then-prevalent standards. The Mummery's Crack on Aiguille du Grépon, which he climbed in 1881, is a stunning 5.7-level climbing site

Table 3.2 The UIAA Mountain Ethics Declaration

1 **Individual responsibility:** Mountaineers and climbers practice their sport in situations where there is a risk of accidents and where outside help may not be available. With this in mind, they engage in this activity at their own risk and are responsible for their own safety. The actions of individuals should not endanger those around them or damage the environment. For example, the fixing of anchors on new or existing routes cannot automatically be taken as acceptable.

2 **Team spirit:** Members of a team should be prepared to make compromises in order to balance the needs and abilities of all in the group. The climb will invariably be most successful where the members support and encourage one another.

3 **Climbing and mountaineering community:** Every person we meet in the mountains or on a rock face deserves an equal measure of respect. Even in remote places and stressful situations, we should always treat others as we want to be treated ourselves.

4 **Visiting foreign countries:** When we are guests in foreign countries, we should always conduct ourselves politely and with restraint. We should show consideration to the local people and their culture – they are our hosts. We should respect local climbing ethics and style and never drill holes or place bolts where there is a traditional ethics against it or where no locally established ethics exists. We will respect holy mountains and other sacred places and always look for ways to benefit and assist local economies and people. An understanding of foreign cultures is part of a complete climbing experience.

5 **Responsibilities of mountain guides and other leaders:** Professional mountain guides, other leaders, and members of the groups they lead should each understand their respective roles and respect the freedoms and rights of other groups and individuals. In this declaration, we recognise the high standards of practice achieved by the mountain guides' own professional body.

6 **Emergencies, dying, and death:** We must be prepared for emergencies and situations which result in serious accidents and death. All participants in mountain sports should clearly understand the risks and hazards and the need to have appropriate skills, knowledge, and equipment. They need to be ready to help others in the event of an emergency or accident and also be ready to face the consequences of a tragedy. It is hoped that commercial operators in particular will warn their clients that their objectives may have to be sacrificed to assist others in distress.

7 **Access and conservation:** We believe that freedom of access to mountains and cliffs in a responsible manner is a fundamental right. We should always practice our activities in an environmentally sensitive way and be proactive in preserving nature and the landscape. We should always respect access restrictions and regulations agreed by climbers with nature conservation organisations and authorities.

8 **Style:** The quality of the experience and how we solve a problem is more important than whether we succeed. We should always strive to leave no trace on the rock face or the mountainside.

(Continued)

9 **First ascents:** The first ascent of a route or a mountain is a creative act. It should be completed in a manner at least as good as the style and traditions of the region. The way the climb was achieved should be reported exactly.

10 **Sponsorship, advertising, and public relations:** The cooperation between sponsors and mountaineers or climbers must be a professional relationship that serves the best interests of mountain sports. It is the responsibility of the mountain sports community to educate and inform both media and the public in a proactive manner.

11 **Use of supplementary oxygen in mountaineering:** The use of supplementary oxygen in high-altitude mountaineering has been under debate for several years. In this debate, different components related to the topic can be distinguished, such as medical aspects and ethical considerations. The medical aspects should be of paramount concern to all mountaineers. Ethical considerations are best left to the individual climber, provided that, if a climber does use oxygen, plans are made to remove used bottles from the mountain.

12 **High-altitude guided commercial expeditions:** It is hoped that commercial operators, especially those without qualifications, attempting 8,000 m or other comparable peaks which offer limited rescue facilities will recognise the limitations of the clients in their care. All efforts should be made to ensure the safety of such clients and also to warn their clients that plans may have to be curtailed to help others on the mountain in distress.

Source: https://www.theuiaa.org/declarations/mountain-ethic-declaration/

that is still not available to everyone. Initial mountaineering guidelines mainly concerned the style of mountaineering and the equipment used. Later on, mountaineers began to consider the impacts of mountaineering on nature and local residents, who often represent ethnic minorities with unique cultural values and ways of life.

Modern codes of mountaineering ethics represent a set of ideals that help mountaineers make decisions about every aspect of mountaineering, including location, mountaineering techniques, and the environment (natural and sociocultural). Consequently, most modern ethical standards are first concerned with the responsibility for mountaineers' actions based on the 'volenti non fit injuria' principle (i.e. voluntary assumption of risk; Stern, 1998). In mountaineering, 'volenti non fit injuria' means that mountaineers willingly accept risks (e.g. on cliffs, mountains, steep paths, or slopes) and are responsible for assessing their actions in terms of the impact that they will have on the interests of others and the environment. Second, mountaineering ethics has a set of rules in relation to environmental protection, caring for the environment to reduce the impact on mountains, paths, and wildlife. Last, ethics in mountaineering is about respect among people. This includes ethics among mountaineers and their support crew, as well as the need to respect the cultural heritage and ways of local mountain communities.

References

Alley, K. D. (1998). Images of waste and purification on the banks of the Ganga. *City & Society, 10*(1), 167–182. https://doi.org/10.1525/city.1998.10.1.167

Andrew, J. D., Nicholas, S. K., Suzy, S., Mark, D. E., Adam, G. W., Hannah, F., Ian, T.-M., & Jon, N. (2009). Determinants of summiting success and acute mountain sickness on Mt Kilimanjaro (5895 m). *Wilderness & Environmental Medicine, 20*(4), 311–317. https://doi.org/10.1580/1080-6032-020.004.0311

Apollo, M. (2010). Anthropopressure mountaineering on the example of Kilimanjaro. In W. Wilczynska-Michalik & R. Gasek (Eds.), *Annales Universitatis Paedagogicae Cracoviensis* (pp. 30–39). Studia Geographica, Pedagogical University in Cracow.

Apollo, M. (2013). Miyar Valley. *American Alpine Journal, 87*(55), 310–311.

Apollo, M. (2015). The clash – Social, environmental and economical changes in tourism destination areas caused by tourism. The case of Himalayan villages (India and Nepal). *Current Issues of Tourism Research, 5*, 6–19.

Apollo, M. (2016). Mountaineer's waste: Past, present and future. Annals of Valahia University of Targoviste, *Geographical Series, 16*(2), 13–32.

Apollo, M. (2017). The true accessibility of mountaineering: The case of the High Himalaya. *Journal of Outdoor Recreation and Tourism, 17*, 29–43. https://doi.org/10.1016/j.jort.2016.12.001

Apollo, M., Andreychouk, V. (2022). *Mountaineering adventure tourism and local communities: Social, environmental and economic interactions.* Cheltenham: Edward Elgar Publishing.

Apollo, M., Mostowska, J., Maciuk,K., Wengel, Y., Jones, T., & Cheer, J. M. (2021). Peak Bagging and Cartographic Misrepresentations. Current Issues in Tourism. 24(14), 1970-1975. https://doi.org/10.1080/13683500.2020.1812541

Apollo, M., Wengel, Y., Schänzel, H., & Musa, G. (2020). Hinduism, ecological conservation, and public health: What are the health hazards for religious tourists at Hindu temples? *Religions, 11*(8), 416. https://doi.org/10.3390/rel11080416

Barber, R. (1993). *Pilgrimages.* The Boydell Press.

Bass, R., Wells, F., & Ridgeway, R. (1986). *Seven summits.* Warner Books.

Borm, N., Van Roo, J. D., Pesce, C., Courtney, D. M., Malik, S., & Lazio, M. P. (2011). Prior altitude experience of climbers attempting to summit Aconcagua. *High Altitude Medicine & Biology, 12*(4), 387–391. https://doi.org/10.1089/ham.2011.1017

Brymer, E. (2013). Extreme sports as transformational tourism. In Y. Reisinger (Ed.), *Transformational tourism: Tourist perspectives* (pp. 111–124). CABI. https://doi.org/10.1079/9781780642093.0000

Casalis, N. (2006). *Stress management in emergency deployment.* World Health Organization.

Csikszentmihalyi, M. (2014). *Flow and the foundations of positive psychology: The collected works of Mihaly Csikszentmihalyi.* Springer Netherlands.

DoT. (2012). *Directorate of tourism.* Dehradun, Uttarakhand

Elmes, M., & Barry, D. (1999). Deliverance, denial, and the death zone: A study of narcissism and regression in the May 1996 Everest climbing disaster. *Journal of Applied Behavioral Science, 35*(2), 163–187. https://doi.org/10.1177/0021886399352003

Eng, R. C. (2010). *Mountaineering: The freedom of the hills.* Mountaineers Books.

Ewert, A. (1985). Why people climb: The relationship of participant motives and experience level to mountaineering. *Journal of Leisure Research, 17*(3), 241–250. https://doi.org/10.1080/00222216.1985.11969634

Ewert, A. (1994). Playing the edge: Motivation and risk taking in a high-altitude wilderness like environment. *Environment and Behavior, 26*(1), 3–24. https://doi.org/10.1177/0013916594261001

Fook, J., Ryan, M., & Hawkins, L. (2000). *Professional expertise: Practice, theory, and education for working in uncertainty.* Whiting & Birch.

Gawlik, A., Apollo, M., Andreychouk, V., & Wengel, Y. (2021). Pilgrimage tourism to sacred places of the high Himalaya. In G. Nyaupane & D. Timothy (Eds.), *Tourism and sustainable development in the Himalayas: Social, environmental, and economic encounters.* Routledge.

Harper, N. J., & Webster, A. L. (2017). Higher learning: Impacts of a high-altitude adventure-based field school on college student development. *Journal of Adventure Education and Outdoor Learning, 17*(1), 67–81. https://doi.org/10.1080/14729679.2016.1217782

Heinrichs, A. (2010). *Mount Everest.* Marshall Cavendish Corp.

Hoibian, O. (2016). A cultural history of mountaineering and climbing. In L. Seifert, P. Wolf, & A. Schweizer (Eds.), *The Science of Climbing and Mountaineering.* Routledge.

Houge Mackenzie, S., & Kerr, J. H. (2012). A (mis)guided adventure tourism experience: An autoethnographic analysis of mountaineering in Bolivia. *Journal of Sport & Tourism, 17*(2), 125–144. https://doi.org/10.1080/14775085.2012.729901

Johnston, B. R., & Edwards, T. (1994). The commodification of mountaineering. *Annals of Tourism Research, 21*(3), 459–478. https://doi.org/10.1016/0160-7383(94)90114-7

Kiełkowska, M., & Kiełkowski, J. (Eds.). (2003). *Wielka encyklopedia gór i alpinizmu.* Wydawnictwo Stapis.

Klemensiewicz, Z. (1937). Turystyka wysokogórska. Główna Księgarnia Wojskowa.

Kottler, J. A. (1998). Transformative travel. *The Futurist, 32*(3), 24 –29.

Kublak, T. (2014). *Mountaineering Methodology – Part 1 – The Basics.* Tomas Kublak – MMPublishing.

Lester, J. (2004). Spirit, identity, and self in mountaineering. *Journal of Humanistic Psychology, 44*(1), 86–100. https://doi.org/10.1177/0022167803257111

Marek, A., & Wieczorek, M. (2015). Tourist traffic in the Aconcagua Massif area. *Quaestiones Geographicae, 34*(3), 65–76. https://doi.org/10.1515/quageo-2015-0022

Maslow, A. H. (1954). *Motivation and personality.* Harper & Row Publishers Inc.

Messerli, B., & Ives, J. (1997). *Mountains of the world: A global priority.* Parthenon Publishing.

Moore, G. P. (2017). Critical incidents in mental health units may be better understood and managed with a Freudian/Lacanian psychoanalytic framework. *European Journal of Psychotherapy & Counselling, 19*(1), 43–60. http://dx.doi.org/10.1080/13642537.2017.1289969

Mu, Y., Nepal, S. K., & Lai, P.-H. (2019). Tourism and sacred landscape in Sagarmatha (Mt. Everest) National Park, Nepal. *Tourism Geographies,* 1–18. https://doi.org/10.1080/14616688.2018.1558454

Musa, G., Hall, C. M., & Higham, J. E. S. (2004). Tourism sustainability and health impacts in high altitude adventure, cultural and ecotourism destinations: A case study of Nepal's Sagarmatha National Park. *Journal of Sustainable Tourism, 12*(4), 306–331. https://doi.org/10.1080/09669580408667240

Nepal, S. K. (2000). Tourism in protected areas: The Nepalese Himalaya. *Annals of Tourism Research, 27*(3), 661–681. https://doi.org/10.1016/S0160-7383(99)00105-X

Nowacki, W. (2009). Góry, partnerstwo, życie – rozmowa z Piotrem Morawskim. *A/Zero – Biuletyn Informacyjno, 16*(1), 8–13.

Okupnik, M. (2002). Wzór kontrkultury alpinistycznej? O narracji autobiograficznej Jerzego Kukuczki. *Idō – Ruch dla Kultury: rocznik naukowy, 3,* 161–178.

Pomfret, G. (2006). Mountaineering adventure tourists: A conceptual framework for research. *Tourism Management, 27*(1), 113–123. https://doi.org/10.1016/j.tourman.2004.08.003

Pomfret, G. (2011). Package mountaineer tourists holidaying in the French Alps: An evaluation of key influences encouraging their participation. *Tourism Management, 32*(3), 501–510. https://doi.org/10.1016/j.tourman.2010.04.001

Pomfret, G. (2012). Personal emotional journeys associated with adventure activities on packaged mountaineering holidays. *Tourism Management Perspectives, 4,* 145–154. https://doi.org/10.1016/j.tmp.2012.08.003

Przecławski, K. (1997). *Człowiek a turystyka. Zarys socjologii turystyki.* Wydawnictwo Albis.

Reisinger, Y. (2013). *Transformational tourism: Tourist perspectives.* CABI. https://doi.org/10.1079/9781780642093.0000

Salisbury, R., & Hawley, E. (2011). *The Himalaya by the numbers: A statistical analysis of mountaineering in the Nepal Himalaya.* Vajra Publications.

Sati, V. P. (2014). *Towards sustainable livelihoods and ecosystems in mountain regions.* Springer.

Sati, V. P. (2015). Pilgrimage tourism in mountain regions: Socio-economic and environmental implications in the Garhwal Himalaya. *South Asian Journal of Tourism and Heritage, 8*(2), 164–182.

Shinde, A. K., Olsen, D. H. (2020). *Religious Tourism and the Environment.* Cabi.

Stepney, P. (2006). Mission impossible? Critical practice in social work 1. Revised version. *The British Journal of Social Work, 36*(8), 1289–1307. https://doi.org/10.1093/bjsw/bch388

Stern, T. (1998). Volenti on high? Voluntary assumption of risk in high risk adventure sports. *Plaintiff* (6), 19–21.

Taylor, S. M. (2007). What if religions had ecologies? The case for reinhabiting religious studies. *Journal for the Study of Religion, Nature and Culture, 1*(1), 129–138. https://doi.org/10.1558/jsrnc.v1i1.129

Thurnell-Read, T. (2017). 'What's on your Bucket List?': Tourism, identity and imperative experiential discourse. *Annals of Tourism Research, 67,* 58–66. https://doi.org/10.1016/j.annals.2017.08.003

Timothy, D. J., & Nyaupane, G. P. (2009). *Cultural heritage and tourism in the developing world: A regional perspective.* Routledge.

Tripp, D. (2011). *Critical incidents in teaching (classic edition) developing professional judgement.* Taylor and Francis.

UIAA. (2009). *Mountain ethics declaration.* https://www.theuiaa.org/declarations/mountain-ethic-declaration/

UNWTO. (1999). *Global code of ethics for tourism.* https://www.unwto.org/global-code-of-ethics-for-tourism

Watling, T. (2009). *Ecological imaginations in the world religions: Ethnographic analysis.* A&C Black.

Wengel, Y., & Apollo, M. (2021). From true mountaineers to mountain tourists: The evolution of mountaineering. *[under review].*

Willig, C. (2008). A phenomenological investigation of the experience of taking part in 'extreme sports'. *Journal of Health Psychology, 13*(5), 690–702. https://doi.org/10.1177/1359105307082459

Zurick, D. N. (1992). Adventure travel and sustainable tourism in the peripheral economy of Nepal. Annal*s of the Association of American Geographers, 82*(4), 608–628. https://doi.org/10.1111/j.1467-8306.1992.tb01720.x

4   Impacts of mountaineering

Abstract

This chapter outlines the impacts of mountaineering in three main categories: environmental impacts, sociocultural impacts, and personal impacts. The consequences of the environmental impacts of mountaineering on the natural environment are characterised by consideration of individual components of the natural environment (land relief, soil, vegetation, fauna, and landscape) and the location/zone of the impact caused by the activity (hiking, trekking, and climbing). In terms of the sociocultural impacts, the chapter discusses the positive and negative changes within mountain communities. Overall, the balance of environmental (natural and socioeconomic) profit and loss depends on several factors and circumstances.

4.1 Environmental impacts of mountaineering

Mountain regions are home to about 25 per cent of the world's terrestrial biodiversity. Mountains have fragile ecosystems, which provide 60–80 per cent of the world's freshwater resources (Palomo, 2017), and they welcome 15–20 per cent of tourists (Debarbieux et al., 2014). Tourism in mountain regions emerged about 200 years ago and increasingly became a primary source of income for many mountain areas. The positive economic impact of tourism in mountain areas ensures that local communities participate directly in the global economy. However, the development of mountaineering and the increasing popularity of tourism in mountain regions also bring many challenges, including significant negative impacts on the environment (Welling et al., 2015).

Any human activity has an impact on the environment, with tourism being one of the largest industries, putting enormous stress on land

DOI: 10.4324/9781003095323-4

use, water resources, and biodiversity. Wilderness areas are the most fragile environments (Buckley, 2000). Mountain regions are therefore susceptible to even slight interference from humans. The world's mountain systems are dynamic and extraordinarily sensitive due to the extreme characteristics of alpine nature (large height differences – sculpture energy, convection, and active exchange of air masses – supply of heat from below, down-flow of cold air) causing high dynamism of geological, geomorphological, hydrological, and climatic processes.

With the development of high-mountain tourism, even locations at the highest altitudes have been exposed to adverse effects. It is difficult to place blame for environmental degradation unequivocally. While the climbing area – accessible only to qualified mountaineers – is damaged only by climbing activities, identifying one key factor in trekking areas is very difficult and it becomes virtually impossible in hiking zones (see Apollo & Andreychouk, 2020a). Underpinned by the models by Wall and Wright (1977) and Barros and Pickering (2015), Apollo (2021) developed a model for the influence of mountaineering on individual elements of the natural environment: soil, land relief, vegetation, wildlife, and water (Figure 4.1).

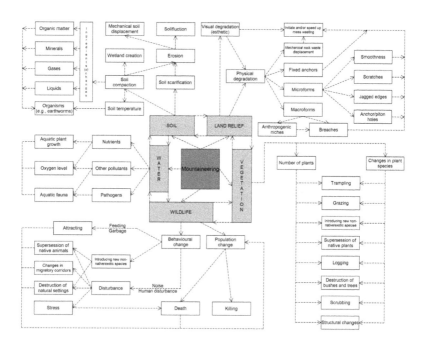

Figure 4.1 Environmental impacts of mountaineering (Apollo, 2021).

4.1.1 Changes in land relief

In terms of **land relief**, the model considers visual and physical degradation. Mountaineering activity increases damage (erosion) to tourist routes (paths and trails) and rock faces (climbing routes), which in turn can accelerate other negative environmental processes. Tourist routes (paths and trails) are the most visible element that transforms the appearance of alpine terrain (Nepal, 2003). In most cases, tourist routes are developed along the most convenient (not necessarily the shortest) terrain (Jodłowski, 2011). The speed of the path creation process depends on the resistance (sensitivity) of the vegetation cover and the number of passes (trampling intensity). At an altitude above 4,000 m in the Himalayas, a path can be created after 1,050–1,175 passes (Apollo & Andreychouk, 2020a).

The most direct impact of mountaineering tourism on the land is the trampling of vegetation, which over time leads to the removal of vegetation cover and the formation of a bare (trodden) surface. Vegetation is directly impacted by hiking on routes and indirectly impacted by all supporting activities (equipment transport, camp infrastructure, etc.). As such, popular mountaineering locations visited by thousands of people per year, such as the New Shira camp (3,766 m) on the Machame Route leading to the top of Kilimanjaro (5,895 m) or the Confluencia base camp (3,390 m) located on the normal route to Aconcagua (6,962 m), show significant changes in the vegetation (and thus the soil cover) at a distance of up to 25 m on average from the camp's borders (Apollo, 2014, 2021). Furthermore, the impact of pack and riding animals on the vegetation on paths is significant (Weaver & Dale, 1978). Due to the total mass of pack animals (deadweight plus load), the damage caused to a trail by a horse is 8 times higher than that caused by a hiker (Cole & Spildie, 1998). According to Barros and Pickering (2015), a pack animal has the same impact on vegetation as 300 tourist passes.

In addition, unpaved paths are most susceptible to deterioration, where the process of erosion (soil, rock rubble, etc.) is accompanied by the exposure of tree roots, subsidence, uncontrolled surface runoff, and widening of the route by creating parallel paths (Hammitt et al., 1998; Leung & Marion, 1996; Marion & Olive, 2006; Tyser & Worley, 1993). For example, existing routes in the Annapurna Conservation Area Project (ACAP) are less damaged than those from Sagarmatha National Park since the main tourist routes in the ACAP region run through villages and are often paved with locally occurring granite (Nepal, 1999, 2003).

Visual or aesthetic deterioration mainly impacts the surface and is caused by footprints, paths, and tent pitches. A further visual impact is the use of chalk and magnesia for climbing. The aesthetic impacts accelerate natural processes. Mechanical displacement and weathering mainly represent physical damage (cutting into the soil, for example) and interference in the rock wall (introducing solid elements, forming micro- and macro-forms). Furthermore, the use of bolts makes climbing safer and more accessible, which can lead to an increasing number of less experienced mountaineers visiting the destination. Environmental impacts on land relief are intensified by the increasing number of tourists participating in mountaineering activities, but although mountaineering stimulates the denudation processes (the set of processes in the destruction of rocks), the impact is marginal.

4.1.2 Changes in soil cover and vegetation

Mountaineering affects **soil** in two different ways: compaction or loosening. Compaction or kneading is a common phenomenon. Trampling from mountaineering activity has a negative effect on the main components of soil (mineral matter, dead organic matter, air, water) and its temperature (change in heat absorption by the changed soil structure), which reduces the soil's biological activity. Compaction limits the soil's water absorption and can lead to swamping of the area. This may occur, for example, slightly above the path on a gently inclined slope. Both loosening (sometimes caused by tent pins) and compaction strengthen terrain denudation processes (natural and mechanical).

One of the most visible and significant impacts of mountaineering is a change in the **vegetation**. Vegetation may be affected by mountaineering directly (by the participants themselves) and also indirectly (by the supporting activities), influencing the population of individual plant species and their diversity. Pescott and Stewart (2014) report that the responses of vegetation to trampling are affected by the following: trampling intensity (number of human trampling passes; see, for example Cole, 1987, 1995a; Whinam & Chilcott, 2003); frequency (trampling passes per time period; Cole & Monz, 2002); distribution (whether trampling passes disperse or clump the soil; Gallet et al., 2004); the weight of broken biomass (Whinam & Chilcott, 2003); the season (Gallet & Roze, 2001); the weather (Gallet & Roze, 2001); the habitat (Chardon et al., 2019; Liddle, 1975); the species (Cole, 1995a; Gallet et al., 2004; Whinam & Chilcott, 2003); Raunkiaer's life-form (perennating bud position) and growth-form (Cole, 1995b); the soil type (Talbot et al., 2003); the surface profile (Whinam & Chilcott, 2003); and the altitude above sea level (Apollo & Andreychouk, 2020b).

Overall, damage to vegetation has a severe impact on the environment as it can negatively affect natural habitats, leading to the loss of vegetation and eventually ground degradation (Fidelus, 2016; Tomczyk & Ewertowski, 2013a, 2013b; Zachar, 2011). For example, trampling in the mountains creates paths that can change plant structures (the size, leaf area, or number of flowers, for instance). Furthermore, seeds carried on the soles of tourists' shoes or in the stools of pack animals may introduce new species that can displace the native species (exotics quickly displace native flora). For example, expedition pack animals graze at lower levels, and their defecation may distribute seeds contained in faeces (Apollo, 2014; Barros et al., 2007; Whinam et al., 1994). Barros and Pickering (2015) state that 21 alien species (mainly originating in Europe) have been introduced in the Horcones Valley (Aconcagua), among which the most prevalent are common bindweed (*Convolvulus arvensis*), dandelion (*Taraxacum officinale F.H. Wigg.*), hedge mustard (*Sisymbrium officinale L. Scop.*), salt cedar (*Tamarix ramosissima*), and five-stems (*Tamarix ramosissima Bunge*).

Furthermore, vegetation is impacted by the pack and riding animals that are used during expeditions. Unfortunately, the use of pack animals is increasing in popularity even in the areas where this did not occur historically. This contributes to soil degradation, which is best evidenced in the works focused on the Andes (Alzérreca et al., 2006; Barros & Pickering, 2014, 2015; Barros et al., 2013; Byers, 2010). Monitoring and control of grazing are essential in protecting species and maintaining biodiversity in high-mountain regions (Cole et al., 2004; Crisfield et al., 2012). For example, the ban on grazing at experimental training grounds in the Horcones Valley (Aconcagua) for just one vegetative period led to a 30 per cent increase in biomass and a two-fold increase in plant height relative to areas under pressure from animals (Barros & Pickering, 2014).

Another issue for vegetation arises when climbers disturb and transform plants growing on rock walls. Usually, the impact on rock-wall vegetation has a linear character which is consistent with the climbing route. Similarly to the impact on vegetation on hiking and trekking routes, the impact on the vegetation on rock walls depends mainly on the intensity of passages and the resistance of plants. The changes caused by climbing are usually mechanical (damage to a plant) or the modification of the structure of a species. Mechanical damage consists mainly of observable changes (a description of visual damage). Changes in the structure of a species of rock plant require specialised comparative studies of, among other things, the modification of the composition of the species and the introduction of new (exotic) plant species. Some of the most common types of degradation that occur because of climbing are the removal of mosses and lichen, damage and removal of rock grasslands, damage to vegetation at the foot of the walls, and damage to trees and shrubs that inhibits successive vegetation (Jodłowski, 2011). Other significant environmental impacts on vegetation include wood felling (e.g. trees and shrubs for fuel), scrubbing (e.g. mechanical removal of mosses and lichens), stopping plant vegetation (e.g. in camps), or damage to bushes and trees. Each of these factors has a significant impact on the vegetation of high mountains.

4.1.3 Faunistic changes

Mountaineering activity and human interference in high-mountain ecosystems have far-reaching effects on **wildlife**. Tourists entering the habitats of wild animals (especially in popular commercialised areas) significantly impact animals' behaviour, which in turn affects their habitats and migration corridors, physical health, and population size (sometimes resulting in the complete displacement or extinction of some species; Beale & Monaghan, 2004; Fennell, 2011; Larm et al., 2018; Usui & Funck, 2018). The growth of adventure tourism brought increased activity levels to natural areas, some of which were previously inhabited by wild animals. Hence, tourism significantly limits foraging areas, disrupts the population, and changes animals' behaviour (Knight & Cole, 1995). Many animals also avoid former feeding areas that are now used for tourism (Gander & Ingold, 1997). For example, when grizzly bears (*Ursus arctos horribilis*) detect human presence in their area, they significantly adjust their behaviours by spending 53 per cent less time feeding, 52 per cent more time navigating the foraging area, and up to 23 per cent more time behaving aggressively compared to those that have not encountered humans (White et al., 1999). This behavioural change indicates the high levels of stress resulting from the presence of tourists. Mountain sheep have been observed to display a much more severe reaction to the presence of tourists than to traffic or aeroplanes or helicopters in flight. Specifically, mountain sheep had a rapidly increased heartrate when they suddenly noticed humans; this jump was even higher when tourists were accompanied by dogs (MacArthur et al., 1982). Similar reactions were demonstrated by the northern chamois (*Rupicapra rupicapra*; Hamr, 1988; Zwijacz-Kozica et al., 2013) and the Pyrenees ibex (*Capra pyrenaica*; Pérez et al., 2002). Disturbances from humans are exceptionally dangerous for animals during the winter when energy demand is higher and food resources are restricted (Cole, 1993; Dorrance et al., 1975; Formenti et al., 2015; Rehnus et al., 2014).

When they encounter animals, humans often attempt to feed them. This practice impacts upon the natural method of foraging, resulting in interdependence on humans, the decline in foraging skills, and, consequently, population decline of dependent species. Furthermore, feeding wild animals can also lead to serious health problems for animals (especially if they are young and still developing) as human food is often nutritionally inadequate. This practice is seen in many natural areas and mountain regions. For example, the endemic mountain parrot, the kea (*Nestor notabilis*), is fed by tourists in the Southern Alps (New Zealand; Gajdon et al., 2006). In the Kilimanjaro massif, the four-striped grass mouse (*Rhabdomys pumilio*) relies on human food (Stewart, 2012), and grizzly bears (*Ursus arctos horribilis*) in the mountains of Alaska or the Rockies break into tents or cars to get food (Gunther et al., 2004). At high altitudes, faunistic changes mainly impact avifauna (Knight & Skagen, 1988; Margalida et al., 2003; Rossi & Knight, 2006). However, it is evidenced that mountaineers also impact the conservation of the Pyrenean ibex (*Capra pyrenaica*; Pérez et al., 2002) and the snail population (McMillan et al., 2003).

4.1.4 Environmental pollution

Mountains play an essential role in providing water, energy, food, and other services to millions of people in the mountains and below. However, many mountainous regions are facing a growing problem with solid waste due to the continued development of urban settlements, the increasingly widespread distribution of consumption patterns (especially tourism), mining, road usage, and illegal dumping practices. The steep incline and remoteness of mountain regions and their socioeconomic conditions and vulnerability to natural hazards make waste management in the mountains even more difficult than in other areas. The effects of gravity and river runoff can also increase the negative impact of waste discharge in the mountains on the environment a 1,000 kilometres or more downstream – right up until it is released into the world's oceans.

Mountaineering tourism impacts all elements of the natural environment of high-mountain areas (air, water, soil, landscape – both visual and acoustic). The main factors leading to environmental pollution are littering, human faecal pollution, and noise or light pollution. Tourism infrastructure is also not without significance, and, together with discarded climbing equipment, it can negatively impact the environment. Littering is caused by improper (accidental or intentional) waste management. The condition of the environment (mainly visual) has a decisive impact on the tourist's perception of the aesthetics (Noe et al., 1997) as well as the choice of tourist destination itself (Godde,

1999). In addition to visual quality (littering of the landscape), littering of the environment affects many elements of nature, including water, soil, and air.

Mountaineers on trekking trips or climbing expeditions contribute to solid waste volumes, especially in more remote and higher mountain regions. As a result of mountaineering tourism, many mountain regions are littered with debris left behind by people on expeditions. This may include, for example, food and its packaging, fuel containers, ropes, used climbing equipment and clothes, batteries, broken glass, 35-mm film packaging, oxygen cylinders, and cooking equipment, including dishes and cutlery. Many remote regions have no adequate waste management systems in place to collect and manage the waste. This is especially evident in mountains of the Global South – particularly where waste is often dumped on the side of trails, at camps or in glacier crevasses, or simply burned.

As Cullen (1986) accurately points out, the chronology of expeditions throughout the entire 20th century can be created by studying the things found at camps. Litter is also hazardous for animate nature, including humans. Dead animals and even the human remains of climbers who have died while climbing (e.g. the body of a mountaineer known as 'Green Boots' on the slopes of Mount Everest) may pose a severe threat to the health of mountaineering participants. Transporting dead animals to a lower altitude is unprofitable so they are often left to deteriorate naturally, risking pollution of the ecosystem. In the case of human bodies of climbers who died during an expedition, their remains are usually located above the death zone and are only accessible to mountaineers. Lifting them requires people who want to make substantial financial and physical investments. For example, the Mount Everest region in Nepal has increasingly received more visitors every year (with 57,289 people visiting Sagarmatha National Park in 2019 alone (Aryal, 2019; Ministry of Culture, Tourism and Civil aviation, 2019), and it is estimated that around 140,000 kilograms of solid waste remains in the region after 60 years of expeditions (Kelliher, 2014). The Government of Nepal works together with the Nepal Mountaineering Association and expedition teams to create regular clean-up campaigns aiming to remove rubbish from mountain slopes (Dangi et al., 2021). Overall, litter and waste management problems are apparent in all mountain regions. However, some reasonable preventive measures and practices exist. These include 'bring-your-waste-back' policies in the Everest and Aconcagua regions, camping and national park fees systems in which profits are redirected to support waste infrastructure, community-based waste initiatives, and successful tourism sector initiatives. To minimise the negative impacts and environmental pollution, it is necessary to implement waste-monitoring programmes in combination with capacity-building and education of mountain communities to raise awareness about waste reduction. The costs of waste collection and removal increase in remote, rough, high-altitude terrain with insufficient waste management infrastructure.

The water stored in high-mountain areas is impacted by climate change and by increasing mountaineering activity in many regions. Mountains and high-altitude regions are linked to lower regions through river systems. These rivers not only bring much-needed water resources but also carry waste produced by mountaineering tourism downstream. Mountaineering impacts **water** resources by introducing pathogens mainly associated with rubbish and human waste. For example, the glacial lakes in close proximity to popular mountaineering sites such as the Everest, Aconcagua, and Kilimanjaro base camps show high levels of nitrate, phosphorous, and algal species (Apollo, 2017; Ells, 1997).

The model described above illustrates the influence of mountaineering tourism on individual elements of the natural environment (Apollo, 2021). Since these elements are interconnected and depend on each other, only comprehensive care for each element can minimise the negative impacts from the mountaineering activity that includes hiking, trekking, and mountain climbing.

4.2 Sociocultural impacts of mountaineering

In some regions, mountains are regarded as divinities or the habitats of spirits that can 'get angry' while in other regions, mountains are just peaks one can climb. Furthermore, mountains directly support the livelihood and well-being of the 1.1 billion people who live in mountain areas and indirectly benefit the billions of people living below by providing tangible (water, energy, and food) and intangible (education and recreation opportunities) resources. The increasing popularity of mountaineering tourism over the past few decades has brought substantial economic development, improved transportation and infrastructure, and significant social change to mountain regions and their unique communities (World Tourism Organization, 2018). Tourism can create prosperity in high-altitude mountain regions, but sustainable development depends on the conservation of natural resources and the participation of local communities. Tourism stakeholders must consider the fragility of mountain ecosystems and strive to preserve the pristine landscapes and healthy environments that make these areas attractive to tourists. For example, with the boom of mountain-based tourism in the 1960s and 1980s, many mountain regions in developed countries (the European Alps, for instance) became overbuilt and overdeveloped and lost their cultural attractiveness (Price et al., 1999).

Previous research has widely examined the popularisation of mountains and the impacts on local residents (Apollo, 2015; Lama & Sattar, 2004; Musa et al., 2004; Serku, 2019). Apollo et al. (2020) highlight that the residents of mountain communities have a greater appreciation of tourism activity and are more reciprocal as the altitude of their habitat increases. However, despite positive economic benefits in remote mountain destinations, researchers agree that the significant cultural and economic gaps between hosts and guests results in substantial degradation of sociocultural heritage and traditions (Lama & Sattar, 2004; Nyaupane & Thapa, 2004; Upadhyay, 2020). Furthermore, local residents point out negative socioeconomic changes resulting from mountaineering tourism, such as pollution, traffic and congestion, noise, and increased living costs (Apollo & Andreychouk, 2021).

Mountaineering tourists often travel in the world's remotest regions, previously cut off from globalisation for several hundred years. While travelling in high-altitude regions, tourists unintentionally display social norms, behaviours, lifestyle, and clothing from a plethora of cultures. The host–guest interaction often results in the popularisation of foreign cultural elements among native people in mountain regions. As such, some locals adopt new clothing styles, lifestyles, pastimes, worldviews, and even foreign word usage in their language.

Although the impacts of mountaineering tourism often threaten the cultural heritage of those living in mountain regions, there is also hope that tourism can be a vehicle for the preservation and maintenance of their unique identity and for sharing it with outsiders by educating tourists about their heritage. As a form of social behaviour, cultures influenced by outside stimulus (e.g. through interactions with tourists) are essentially inclined to change; however, at the same time, cultures can resist change. Stevens (1991) notices that despite the influence of tourism in the Mount Everest region the Sherpa community shows cultural continuity with deliberate maintenance of many cultural aspects related to the community's fundamental values, beliefs, subsistence practices, and lifestyle.

Social interactions, new technologies, and exposure to the outside world brought by tourists can produce changes within ethnic communities in mountain regions; however, mountain communities should be empowered to embrace new ideas and trends that could allow them to improve their knowledge and skills in order to participate in a beneficial host–guest exchange. In the long term, the unique cultural heritage of mountain communities is one of the key elements attracting mountaineering tourists. Hence, the communities (including individuals, entrepreneurs, community groups, and representatives of the government) should work together towards not only cultural preservation but also empowerment and the acquisition of skills to manage ever-changing tourism demand sustainably.

4.3 A comprehensive approach to the mountaineering–environment relationship

The relationship between mountaineering tourism and the environment, and also its impact, is usually considered in the context of tourists and their friendly or hostile interactions with animated and inanimate nature (Apollo, 2021). A comprehensive assessment of the impact is not possible without a profound understanding of the high-altitude mountain environment and its systematic nature. Commonly, a geographic (mountain) ecosystem is complex and includes different elements of nature (abiotic, biotic, anthropic, etc.), which are interconnected to each other on several levels, therefore creating the entire system (Andreychouk, 2015). External influences on this system are relatively stable, but a sensitive mountain geosystem provokes a series of reactions (internal interactions), leading to various changes that can be perceived as being positive, negative, or neutral.

Mountaineering activity is being held responsible for the degradation of high-altitude mountain environments, and assessing the impacts on the fragile geosystem is not possible without seeing the interplay of actors and the system as a whole. Apollo and Andreychouk (2021) present a comprehensive, holistic approach to assessing the environmental impacts of mountaineering.

Depending on the region and developmental conditions, the changes occurring from mountaineering tourism can have both negative and positive implications. Figure 4.2 and its description below present a simplified image of the evolution of the high-mountain environment due to mountaineering development (Apollo, 2015; Apollo & Andreychouk, 2020a).

Historically, in the early stages of contemporary mountaineering in the middle of the 20th century, 'elite mountaineering' (not a mass phenomenon) appeared in the high-altitude mountain areas. These few experienced mountaineers were aware of the natural and cultural changes they had introduced; therefore, their impact was deemed to be marginal. At this stage, local communities mainly focused on traditional activities to sustain their living, such as crop growing and husbandry (traditional labour-consuming agriculture). Population growth leads to expenditure in agricultural areas. Hence, the pressure

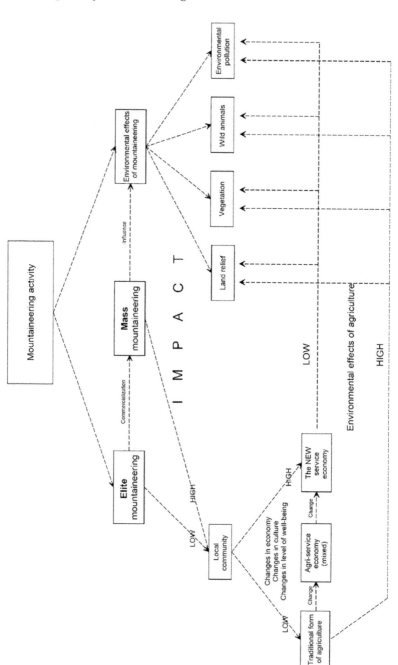

Figure 4.2 Model of the environmental effects of mountaineering in developing countries (Apollo & Andreychouk, 2020a).

on fragile high-altitude mountain environments increased too. However, with the popularisation of mountaineering, the local population (often living in economically deprived mountain regions in the Global South) recognised the economic opportunities (from mountaineering activity), which in turn led to the development of *in situ* services at every stage of the expedition (see Chapter 2).

With the shift from traditional agriculture as the primary means of income to an agriservices mixed economy, the negative impacts from agriculture on the environment decreased. As mountaineering became increasingly popular and the number of mountaineering tourists and

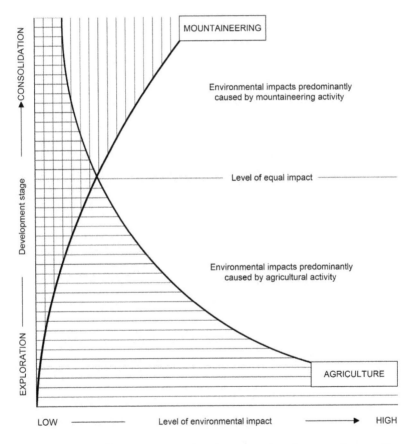

Figure 4.3 Qualitative model showing the comparison between the transformation level of the natural environment under the influence of (a) agriculture and (b) mountaineering, relative to the development stages of tourism (Apollo & Andreychouk, 2020a).

tourism services grew, consumption and commerce became increasingly important in mountain regions. In the contemporary stage of mountaineering (since 1964), mountaineering became a mass activity with organised expeditions on Everest starting in the 1990s. Since that time, mountain communities' economies have predominantly focused on services related to mountaineering tourism, and agriculture has become a secondary industry. Agricultural activity in many (even developed) regions reduced to ensure self-sufficiency (kitchen gardens, for instance) of the local population and cater to tourist needs. Over time, mass mountaineering started to have a higher environmental impact than agriculture. Figure 4.3 illustrates the order of development described above. It fits into the concept of Butler's tourism area lifecycle.

It should be noted that mountaineering always impacts the natural environment within populated high-mountain areas, contrary to widespread opinion. Although mountaineering itself – as with any other kind of touristic activity – usually results in some kind of losses within the natural environment, one should always consider the balance of benefits and losses. Mountaineering supersedes traditional farming; the indisputably negative impact of agriculture on all components of the natural environment decreases. In turn, shrinking farmland acreage and decline in livestock numbers significantly increase the land available for wild animals and allow space for wild plants to recover (from herding, for instance). Therefore, mountaineering may support the gradual regeneration of vegetation and animal habitats and a growing diversity of flora and fauna species.

In the high-altitude mountain environment (above the populated areas and herding areas), mountaineering has negative impacts on the natural environment. However, the scale of the impact that mountaineering has on the natural environment should be taken into consideration as it accounts for just a tiny percentage of the changes that occur in the high-altitude natural environment. Consequently, attaching great importance to mountaineering when studying environmental conditions seems to be unjustified.

Mountaineering tourism can provide an alternative economic opportunity to the areas where locals suspend traditional agriculture. The additional income from tourism affects economic structures and contributes to a shift from agricultural activities towards part-time farming (Uhlig & Kreutzmann, 1995). Furthermore, tourism development reduces farmland area and the number of herding animals (Apollo, 2015), diminishing the pressure from human activity in the high-altitude mountain environment. It is not always the case that local people who have adopted tourism and have earned money from it use the opportunity to reduce their agricultural activities (Yang et al., 2009). Therefore, tourism development should be accompanied by relevant, sustainable development policies suitable for mountain regions.

References

Alzérreca, H., Laura, J., Loza, F., Luna, D., & Ortega, J. (2006). Importance of Carrying Capacity in sustainable management of key high-Andean Puna rangelands (bofedales) in Ulla Ulla, Bolivia. In E. M. Spehn, M. Liberman, & C. Körner (Eds.), *Land use change and mountain biodiversity*, (pp. 167–185). CRC Press.

Andreychouk, V. (2015). Cultural landscape functions. In: M. Luc, U. Somorowska, & J.B. Szmańda (Eds.), *Landscape analysis and planning* (s. 3–19). Springer.

Apollo, M. (2014). Climbing as a kind of human impact on the high mountain environment – based on the selected peaks of Seven Summits. *Journal of Selcuk University Natural and Applied Science, 2014*(2), 1061–1071.

Apollo, M. (2015). The clash – social, environmental and economical changes in tourism destination areas caused by tourism. The case of Himalayan villages (India and Nepal). *Current Issues of Tourism Research, 5*, 6–19.

Apollo, M. (2017). The good, the bad and the ugly–three approaches to management of human waste in a high-mountain environment. *International Journal of Environmental Studies, 74*(1), 129–158. https://doi.org/10.1080/00207233.2016.1227225

Apollo, M. (2021). *Environmental impacts of mountaineering: A conceptual framework*. Springer.

Apollo, M., & Andreychouk, V. (2020a). Mountaineering and the natural environment in developing countries: An insight to a comprehensive approach. *International Journal of Environmental Studies, 77*(6), 942–953. https://doi.org/10.1080/00207233.2019.1704047

Apollo, M., & Andreychouk, V. (2020b). Trampling Intensity and Vegetation Response and Recovery according to Altitude: An Experimental Study from the Himalayan Miyar Valley. *Resources, 9*(8), 98. https://doi.org/10.3390/resources9080098

Apollo, M. & Andreychouk, V. (2022). Mountaineering adventure tourism and local communities: Social, environmental and economic interactions. Cheltenham: Edward Elgar Publishing.

Apollo, M., Andreychouk, V., Moolio, P., Wengel, Y., & Myga-Piątek, U. (2020). Does the altitude of habitat influence residents' attitudes to guests? A new dimension in the residents' attitudes to tourism. *Journal of Outdoor Recreation and Tourism, 31*, 100312. https://doi.org/10.1016/j.jort.2020.100312

Aryal, P. (2019). *Nepal tourism statistics 2018*. Ministry of Culture, Tourism & Civil Aviation, Kathmandu, Nepal, available at: https://tourism.gov.np/files/statistics/19.pdf (accessed 23 February 2020).

Barros, A., Berlanga, P., & Prause, P. (2007). Buenas Prácticas para la Conservación de Ecosistemas de Montaña. In J. Junquera, E. Natale, P. Prause, & A. Barros (Eds.), *Capacitacion de guías turísticos del monument natural Puente Del Inca y Laguna De Los Horcones* (Parque Provincial Aconcagua) (pp. 185–218). Dirección de Recursos Naturales Renovables de Mendoza.

Barros, A., Gonnet, J., & Pickering, C. (2013). Impacts of informal trails on vegetation and soils in the highest protected area in the Southern Hemisphere. *Journal of Environmental Management, 127*, 50–60. https://doi.org/10.1016/j.jenvman.2013.04.030

Barros, A., & Pickering, C. M. (2014). Non-native plant invasion in relation to tourism use of Aconcagua Park, Argentina, the highest protected area in the southern hemisphere. *Mountain Research and Development, 34*(1), 13–26. https://doi.org/10.1659/MRD-JOURNAL-D-13-00054.1

Barros, A., & Pickering, C. M. (2015). Impacts of experimental trampling by hikers and pack animals on a high-altitude alpine sedge meadow in the Andes. *Plant Ecology and Diversity, 8*(2), 265–276. https://doi.org/10.1080/17550874.2014.893592

Beale, C. M., & Monaghan, P. (2004). Behavioural responses to human disturbance: A matter of choice? *Animal Behaviour, 68*(5), 1065–1069. https://doi.org/10.1016/j.anbehav.2004.07.002

Buckley, R. (2000). Tourism in the most fragile environments. *Tourism Recreation Research, 25*(1), 31–40. https://doi.org/10.1080/02508281.2000.11014898

Byers, A. (2010). *Recuperación de pastos alpinos en el valle de Ishinca, Parque Nacional del Huascarán, Perú: Implicaciones para la conservación, las comunidades y el cambio climático.* Instituto de Montaña. www.keneamazon.net/Documents/Publications/Virtual-Library/Ecosistemas.../5.pdf

Chardon, N. I., Rixen, C., Wipf, S., & Doak, D. F. (2019). Human trampling disturbance exerts different ecological effects at contrasting elevational range limits. *Journal of Applied Ecology, 56*(6), 1389–1399. https://doi.org/10.1111/1365-2664.13384

Cole, D. N. (1987). Effects of three seasons of experimental trampling on five montane forest communities and a grassland in Western Montana, USA. *Biological Conservation, 40*(3), 219–244. https://doi.org/10.1016/0006-3207(87)90087-5

Cole, D. N. (1993). Minimizing conflict between recreation and nature conservation. In D. S. H. P. C. Smith (Ed.), *Ecology of greenways: Design and function of linear conservation areas* (pp. 105–122). University of Minnesota Press.

Cole, D. N. (1995a). Experimental trampling of vegetation. I. relationship between trampling intensity and vegetation response. *The Journal of Applied Ecology, 32*(1), 203–203. https://doi.org/10.2307/2404429

Cole, D. N. (1995b). Experimental trampling of vegetation. II. Predictors of resistance and resilience. *Journal of Applied Ecology, 32*, 215–224. https://doi.org/10.1016/0006-3207(96)83222-8

Cole, D. N., & Monz, C. A. (2002). Trampling disturbance of high-elevation vegetation, Wind River Mountains, Wyoming, U.S.A. *Arctic, Antarctic, and Alpine Research, 34*(4), 365–376. https://doi.org/10.2307/1552194

Cole, D. N., & Spildie, D. R. (1998). Hiker, horse and llama trampling effects on native vegetation in Montana, USA. *Journal of Environmental Management, 53*(1), 61–71. https://doi.org/10.1006/jema.1998.0192

Cole, D. N., Van Wagtendonk, J. W., McClaran, M. P., Moore, P. E., & McDougald, N. K. (2004). Response of mountain meadows to grazing by recreational pack stock. *Journal of Range Management, 57*(2), 153–160. https://doi.org/10.2111/1551-5028(2004)057[0153:rommtg]2.0.co;2

Crisfield, V., MacDonald, S., & Gould, A. (2012). Effects of recreational traffic on alpine plant communities in the northern Canadian Rockies. *Arctic, Antarctic, and Alpine Research, 44*(3), 277–287. https://doi.org/10.1657/1938-4246-44.3.277

Cullen, R. (1986). Himalayan mountaineering expedition garbage. *Environmental Conservation, 13*(4), 293–297. https://doi.org/10.1017/S0376892900035335

Dangi, T., Birendra, K. C., & Gautam, L. (2021). History of tourism planning and development in Nepal: Achievements and challenges to sustainable future tourism. In D. Stylidis & B. Seetanah (Eds.), *Tourism planning and development in South Asia* (pp. 42–62). CABI.

Debarbieux, B., Oiry Varacca, M., Rudaz, G., Maselli, D., Kohler, T., & Jurek, M. (2014). *Tourism in mountain regions: Hopes, fears and realities Sustainable Mountain Development Series.* UNIGE, CDE, SDC.

Dorrance, M. J., Savage, P. J., & Huff, D. E. (1975). Effects of snowmobiles on white-tailed deer. *The Journal of Wildlife Management, 39*(3), 563–563. https://doi.org/10.2307/3800399

Ells, M. D. (1997).Impact of Human Waste Disposal on Surface Water Runoff The Muir Snowfield, Mount Rainier. *Journal of Environmental Health, 59(8)*, 6–12. http://www.jstor.org/stable/44533135

Fennell, D. A. (2011). *Tourism and animal ethics.* Routledge.

Fidelus, J. (2016). Slope transformations within tourist footpaths in the northern and southern parts of the Western Tatra Mountains (Poland, Slovakia). *Zeitschrift fur Geomorphologie, 60*, 139–152. https://doi.org/10.1127/zfg_suppl/2016/00265

Formenti, N., Viganó, R., Bionda, R., Ferrari, N., Trogu, T., Lanfranchi, P., & Palme, R. (2015). Increased hormonal stress reactions induced in an alpine black Grouse (Tetrao tetrix) population by winter sports. *Journal of Ornithology, 156*(1), 317–321. https://doi.org/10.1007/s10336-014-1103-3

Gajdon, G. K., Fijn, N., & Huber, L. (2006). Limited spread of innovation in a wild parrot, the kea (Nestor notabilis). *Animal Cognition, 9*(3), 173–181. https://doi.org/10.1007/s10071-006-0018-7

Gallet, S., Lemauviel, S., & Roze, F. (2004). Responses of three heathland shrubs to single or repeated experimental trampling. *Environmental Management, 33*(6), 821–829. https://doi.org/10.1007/s00267-004-0017-x

Gallet, S., & Roze, F. (2001). Resistance of Atlantic Heathlands to trampling in Brittany (France): Influence of vegetation type, season and weather conditions. *Biological Conservation, 97*(2), 189–198. https://doi.org/10.1016/S0006-3207(00)00111-7

Gander, H., & Ingold, P. (1997). Reactions of male alpine chamois Rupicapra r. rupicapra to hikers, joggers and mountainbikers. *Biological Conservation, 79*(1), 107–109. https://doi.org/10.1016/S0006-3207(96)00102-4

Godde, P. M. (1999). *Tourism and development in mountain regions.* CABI. https://doi.org/10.1079/9780851993911.0000

Gunther, K., Haroldson, M., Frey, K., Cain, S., Copeland, C., & Schwartz, C. (2004). Grizzly bear–human conflicts in the Greater Yellowstone ecosystem, 1992–2000. *Ursus, 15*(1). https://doi.org/10.2192/1537-6176(2004)015<0010:GBCITG>2.0.CO;2

Hammitt, W. E., Cole, D. N., & Monz, C. A. (1998). *Wildland recreation: Ecology and management.* Hoboken, John Wiley and Sons.

Hamr, J. (1988). Disturbance behaviour of chamois in an Alpine tourist area of Austria. *Mountain Research & Development, 8*(1), 65–73. https://doi.org/10.2307/3673407

Jodłowski, M. (2011). *Zasady dobrej praktyki w zarządzaniu ruchem wspinaczkowym na obszarach chronionych.* Wydawnictwo Uniwersytetu Jagiellońskiego.

Kelliher, K. (2014). *An examination of governmental and nongovernmental organizations in Nepal: A partnership in managing and eliminating waste in the Solukhumbu.* https://digitalcollections.sit.edu/isp_collection/1964

Knight, R. L., & Cole, D. N. (1995). Wildlife responses to climate change. In R. L. Knight & K. Gutzwiller (Eds.), (pp. 51–69). Wildlife and recreationists: Coexistence through management and research. Washington, DC: Island Press.

Knight, R. L., & Skagen, S. K. (1988). Agonistic asymmetries and the foraging ecology of bald eagles. *Ecology, 69*(4), 1188–1194. https://doi.org/10.2307/1941273

Lama, W. B., & Sattar, N. (2004). Mountain tourism and the conservation of biological and cultural diversity. In M. Price, L. Jansky, & A. Iatsenia (Eds.), *Key issues for mountain areas* (pp. 111–148). Tokyo: United Nations University Press.

Larm, M., Elmhagen, B., Granquist, S. M., Brundin, E., & Angerbjörn, A. (2018). The role of wildlife tourism in conservation of endangered species: Implications of safari tourism for conservation of the Arctic fox in Sweden. *Human Dimensions of Wildlife, 23*(3), 257–272. https://doi.org/10.1080/10871209.2017.1414336

Leung, Y. F., & Marion, J. L. (1996). Trail degradation as influenced by environmental factors: A state-of-the-knowledge review. *Journal of Soil and Water Conservation, 51*(2), 130–136. http://pubs.er.usgs.gov/publication/5223256

Liddle, M. J. (1975). A theoretical relationship between the primary productivity of vegetation and its ability to tolerate trampling. *Biological Conservation, 8*(4), 251–255. https://doi.org/10.1016/0006-3207(75)90002-6

MacArthur, R. A., Geist, V., & Johnston, R. H. (1982). Cardiac and Behavioral Responses of Mountain Sheep to Human Disturbance. *The Journal of Wildlife Management, 46*(2), 351–351. https://doi.org/10.2307/3808646

Margalida, A., Garcia, D., Bertran, J., & Heredia, R. (2003). Breeding biology and success of the Bearded Vulture Gypaetus barbatus in the eastern Pyrenees. *Ibis, 145*(2), 244–252. https://doi.org/10.1046/j.1474-919X. 2003.00148.x

Marion, J. L., & Olive, N. (2006). *Assessing and understanding trail degradation: Results from Big South Fork National River and recreational area.* Reston, VA: US Geological Survey. http://pubs.er.usgs.gov/publication/5200309.

McMillan, M. A., Nekola, J. C., & Larson, D. W. (2003). Effects of rock climbing on the land snail community of the Niagara Escarpment in southern Ontario, Canada. *Conservation Biology, 17*(2), 616–621. https://doi. org/10.1046/j.1523-1739.2003.01362.x

Musa, G., Hall, C. M., & Higham, J. E. S. (2004). Tourism sustainability and health impacts in high altitude adventure, cultural and ecotourism destinations: A case study of Nepal's Sagarmatha National Park. *Journal of Sustainable Tourism, 12*(4), 306–331. https://doi.org/10.1080/ 09669580408667240

Nepal, S. K. (1999). *Tourism-induced environmental change in the Nepalese Himalaya: A comparative analysis of the Everest Annapurna and Mustang Region* University of Berne]. Berne. https://lib.icimod.org/record/190

Nepal, S. K. (2003). *Tourism and the environment perspectives from the Nepal Himalaya.* Himal Books.

Noe, F. P., Hammitt, W. E., & Bixler, R. D. (1997). Park user perceptions of resource and use impacts under varied situations in three national parks. *Journal of Environmental Management, 49*(3), 323–336. https://doi. org/10.1006/jema.1995.0093

Nyaupane, G. P., & Thapa, B. (2004). Evaluation of ecotourism: A comparative assessment in the Annapurna Conservation Area Project, Nepal. *Journal of Ecotourism, 3*(1), 20–45. https://doi.org/10.1080/14724040408668148

Palomo, I. (2017). Climate change impacts on ecosystem services in high mountain areas: A literature review. *Mountain Research and Development, 37*(2), 179–187, 179. https://doi.org/10.1659/MRD-JOURNAL-D-16-00110.1

Pérez, J. M., Granados, J. E., Soriguer, R. C., Fandos, P., Márquez, F. J., & Crampe, J. P. (2002). Distribution, status and conservation problems of the Spanish Ibex, Capra pyrenaica (Mammalia: Artiodactyla). *Mammal Review, 32*(1), 26–39. https://doi.org/10.1046/j.1365-2907.2002.00097.x

Pescott, O. L., & Stewart, G. B. (2014). Assessing the impact of human trampling on vegetation: A systematic review and meta-analysis of experimental evidence. *PeerJ, 2014*(1). https://doi.org/10.7717/peerj.360

Price, M., Wachs, T., & Byers, E. (1999). *Mountains of the world: Tourism and sustainable mountain development.* Institute of Geography, University of Berne.

Rehnus, M., Wehrle, M., & Palme, R. (2014). Mountain hares Lepus timidus and tourism: Stress events and reactions. *Journal of Applied Ecology, 51*(1), 6–12. https://doi.org/10.1111/1365-2664.12174

Rossi, L. G., & Knight, R. L. (2006). Cliff attributes and bird communities in Jefferson County, Colorado. *Natural Areas Journal, 26*(4), 331–338. https:// doi.org/10.3375/0885-8608(2006)26[331:CAABCI]2.0.CO;2

Serku, S. (2019). *Sherpa Samudayako Maulik Pahichan [The identity of Sherpa's community]*. Jagadamba Press Pvt. Ltd.

Stevens, S. F. (1991). Sherpas, Tourism, and cultural change in Nepal's Mount Everest region. *Journal of Cultural Geography, 12*(1), 32–58. https://doi.org/10.1080/08873639109478419

Stewart, A. (2012). *Kilimanjaro – A complete trekker's guide: Preparations, practicalities and trekking routes to the 'Roof of Africa'*. Cicerone Press Ltd.

Talbot, L. M., Turton, S. M., & Graham, A. W. (2003). Trampling resistance of tropical rainforest soils and vegetation in the wet tropics of north east Australia. *Journal of Environmental Management, 69*(1), 63–69. https://doi.org/10.1016/S0301-4797(03)00119-1

Tomczyk, A. M., & Ewertowski, M. (2013a). Planning of recreational trails in protected areas: Application of regression tree analysis and geographic information systems. *Applied Geography, 40*, 129–139. https://doi.org/10.1016/j.apgeog.2013.02.004

Tomczyk, A. M., & Ewertowski, M. (2013b). Quantifying short-term surface changes on recreational trails: The use of topographic surveys and 'digital elevation models of differences' (DODs). *Geomorphology, 183*, 58–72. https://doi.org/10.1016/j.geomorph.2012.08.005

Tyser, R. W., & Worley, C. A. (1993). Alien flora in grasslands adjacent to road and trail corridors in Glacier National Park, Montana, (USA). *Biological Conservation, 64*(2), 179–179. https://doi.org/10.1016/0006-3207(93)90688-w

Uhlig, H., & Kreutzmann, H. (1995). Persistence and change in high mountain agricultural systems. *Mountain Research and Development, 15*, 199. https://doi.org/10.2307/3673928

Upadhyay, P. (2020). Tourist-host interactions and tourism experiences: A study of tourism experiences and effects in Sikles, Nepal. *The Gaze: Journal of Tourism and Hospitality, 11*(1), 81–106. https://doi.org/10.3126/gaze.v11i1.26619

Usui, R., & Funck, C. (2018). Analysing food-derived interactions between tourists and sika deer (Cervus nippon) at Miyajima Island in Hiroshima, Japan: Implications for the physical health of deer in an anthropogenic environment. *Journal of Ecotourism, 17*(1), 67–78. https://doi.org/10.1080/14724049.2017.1421641

Wall, G., & Wright, C. (1977). *The environmental impact of outdoor recreation*. Department of Geography, Faculty of Environmental Studies, University of Waterloo.

Weaver, T., & Dale, D. (1978). Trampling effects of hikers, motorcycles and horses in meadows and forests. *The Journal of Applied Ecology, 15*(2), 451–451. https://doi.org/10.2307/2402604

Welling, J. T., Árnason, Þ., & Ólafsdottír, R. (2015). Glacier tourism: A scoping review. *Tourism Geographies, 17*(5), 635–662. https://doi.org/10.1080/14616688.2015.1084529

Whinam, J., Cannell, E. J., Kirkpatrick, J. B., & Comfort, M. (1994). Studies on the potential impact of recreational horseriding on some alpine environments of the central plateau, Tasmania. *Journal of Environmental Management, 40*(2), 103–117. https://doi.org/10.1006/jema.1994.1007

Whinam, J., & Chilcott, N. M. (2003). Impacts after four years of experimental trampling on alpine/sub-alpine environments in western Tasmania. *Journal of Environmental Management, 67*(4), 339–351. https://doi.org/10.1016/S0301-4797(02)00218-9

White, D., Kendall, K. C., & Picton, H. D. (1999). Potential energetic effects of mountain climbers on foraging grizzly bears. *Wildlife Society Bulletin, 27*(1), 146–151.

World Tourism Organization. (2018). *Sustainable Mountain Tourism – Opportunities for Local Communities, Executive Summary.* UNWTO. https://doi.org/10.18111/9789284420261

Yang, M., Hens, L., Ou, X., & De Wulf, R. (2009). Tourism: An alternative to development? Reconsidering farming, tourism, and conservation incentives in Northwest Yunnan mountain communities. *Mountain Research and Development, 29*(1), 75–81. https://doi.org/10.1659/mrd.1051

Zachar, D. (2011). *Soil erosion.* Elsevier. https://doi.org/10.1017/CBO978051 1807527.014

Zwijacz-Kozica, T., Selva, N., Barja, I., Silván, G., Martínez-Fernández, L., Illera, J. C., & Jodłowski, M. (2013). Concentration of fecal cortisol metabolites in chamois in relation to tourist pressure in Tatra National Park (South Poland). *Acta Theriologica, 58*(2), 215–222. https://doi.org/10.1007/s13364-012-0108-7

5 Management practices in mountain regions

Abstract

This chapter provides a brief overview of existing management practices in mountain regions. It presents current policies that work well (including a range of examples and approaches) and focuses on acclimatisation and disaster response materials. In addition, it highlights some policies that require further development and improvement for sustainable management of mountain regions and mountaineering tourism activity. Finally, it presents guidelines on the natural environment and local communities, providing the foundation for further management plans. Implementation of the plans should consist of (1) development of even more specific guidelines, (2) communication, (3) education, (4) monitoring, and (5) conducting (physical) preservation measures.

5.1 Existing management practices in mountain regions

Climbing in a given area is often regulated by laws and regulations resulting from higher-order nature protection regulations (Jodłowski, 2011; Bui et al., 2021; Jones et al., 2021). Protected areas are an exception (e.g. National Parks and Reserves), but even in those settings, usually, only values pertaining to the natural environment are regulated. Thus, the protection of the local population is completely forgotten. Frequently, aspects of their lives such as culture and customs are overlooked. In many mountain regions (not protected), mountain tourists participate in both aspects (natural and social), following self-established general rules. These rules often coincide with the ethical values adhered to by elite mountaineers who eventually popularised this recreation activity. They follow the well-established principles of 'Leave No Trace' or 'Pack It In, Pack It Out', which aim to leave

DOI: 10.4324/9781003095323-5

no impact on the natural environment. Unfortunately, self-control ceases to be sufficient when mass tourism appears. To this day, rules about communicating with people from other cultures, appropriate for the natural environment, have not been developed. None of the generally accepted principles (even if they arise) will result in 100 per cent effectiveness. This thesis particularly applies to areas with a high protection regime. High-altitude mountain regions – both in terms of the natural environment and local communities – are a perfect example in which only specific guidelines (rules) adjusted to environmental specifications will bring the desired effect. In many areas, specific management plans are prepared under certain conditions; they contribute to achieving the set goal. In the case of mountaineering, this goal is to reduce the negative impacts of participants on the broadly understood alpine environment while maintaining development. However, as mentioned in the introduction, tourism-generating development in the reception area and the changes that follow from it are viewed from the perspectives of residents who derive measurable benefits from it, tourists, or researchers. It is extremely easy to fall into the temptation to create, or at least evaluate, local communities following a pro-Western vision.

Globally, most tourists come from developed countries, but many receiving countries are classified as emerging economies. It is they (the receiving countries) that are most exposed to sociocultural and natural changes the more so because, as numerous studies show, tourists behave differently when on holiday (Przecławski, 1997). Many tourists not only do not respect the social and cultural values of the local population – as this research has also shown – but even treat their trip as an exemption from the obligation to observe moral and social norms in their living environment (Nettekoven, 1972; Reisinger & Turner, 2003; Kozak & Tasci, 2005; Apollo, 2015). Xenophobic behaviour will lead to isolation or internal conflicts (closure). On the other hand, the wide infiltration of norms from other cultures leads to the blurring of one's own identity (opening; Przecławski, 1997).

Furthermore, conservation programmes often run counter to the local community's economic goals (Apollo, 2015; Apollo & Andreychouk, 2022). The concept of sustainable tourism is pushed in the countries of the North (West) as a form of tourism development, management, and tourism activities that maintains the ecological and socioeconomic cohesion of the area and preserves its natural and cultural resources in opposition to the development goals of the communities behind the so-called Brandt Line, also known as the Global South. In practice, the integration of tourism activities with environmental protection objectives and a lack of negative ethical and social changes in the local population is possible only with a small number of tourists and, therefore, with lower income generation for the community (Apollo & Andreychouk, 2022). Although the intent is good (and right for the countries of the North), the assumptions of sustainable tourism block the development of the countries of the South (Apollo, 2015; Craig-Smith & French, 1994). It is only by creating an individual management plan that the demands of each entity directly and indirectly affected by tourism activities can be taken into account. Therefore, it is imperative to know the position of each entity, including the residents of the reception area, on tourism and the tourists themselves, since negative attitudes in the local community may hinder its development (Williams & Lawson, 2001; Yun & Zhang, 2017). This is essential because there is a multifaceted collision between high-mountain environments (natural and local communities) that have been cut off for many years and mountaineering and the globalisation that it brings (Apollo, 2015; Apollo & Andreychouk, 2022).

5.2 A mountaineering management model

A high-mountain-climbing tourism traffic management plan should be developed separately for each region, each time taking into account the elements of an extremely sensitive and unique environment. This uniqueness is exhibited in the characteristics of the high-mountain areas of the Himalayas and the human living environments. A mountaineering management plan should be developed with cooperation between the government administration, local governments, nature conservation services, pro-environmental organisations, scientific institutions, tour operators, and mountaineering tourism organisations and their participants (see Figure 5.1).

The above entities must cooperate to consider each of the objectives, and the plan should be built on consensus. The process of reaching consensus requires the community to consider and take seriously the opinions of each member. This is of great importance because, as shown in the works devoted exclusively to climbing, the lack of consultations with climbing communities and the climbers themselves about the regulations that directly affect them is something they often contest (Jodłowski, 2010, 2011; Monz, 2009; Waldrup & McEwen, 1994). A detailed inventory and valorisation should precede the discourse by the various entities. The inventory and valorisation should consider the specifications of the natural environment and human communities, the type of alpine activities on offer, the attractiveness of the region,

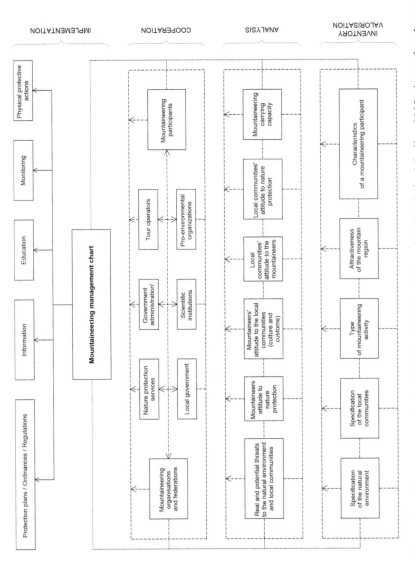

Figure 5.1 Mountaineering management chart (elaborated after Jodłowski, 2011; Pyke & Iodice, 2008; also authors' own research).

and the characteristics of the participants. The collected data should then be thoroughly analysed on the basis of the actual and potential threats to the natural environment and human communities and the tourist capacity of the region. Managers should also analyse the relationship (existing and anticipated) between the local population and the mountaineering participants. The relations between both groups in terms of environmental protection should be critically looked at, emphasising regions belonging to developing countries. Conclusions from the conducted analyses should be collected into a mountaineering traffic management plan, and the document should be approved by all entities concerned.

The region may be made available for tourists based on the guidelines contained in the plan. Site management should be under the constant control of representatives of each of the groups concerned. Managers should take action in the order outlined below as these steps will only work if coordinated. The correct implementation of the plan should be based on:

1   Developing more detailed guidelines (protection plans, ordinances, regulations) – their introduction should be preceded by consultations with interested entities so that changes (restrictions) do not affect only one of the parties involved.
2   Informing – all guidelines should be coherent and unambiguous and clearly communicated. Information on standards of conduct and the consequences of noncompliance should be made widely available through various information outlets, including on websites, boards and signs, and in guides.
3   Educating – each party should be educated on an ongoing basis about the gains and losses of the policy pursued. Information alone, without educational policy, may not meet the approval of the parties concerned.
4   Monitoring – the area should be closely monitored in order to prevent all deviations from the adopted plan in time (hasty improvement of one element may lead to a negative reflection in another).
5   Introducing (physical) protective measures – as a last resort, introduce physical measures to counteract change. These may involve, for example, improving the trail or reducing the number of tourists. Having all entities that participate in mountaineering create one common traffic management plan provides the best opportunity to maintain sustainable development. Not all management tasks are aimed at stopping or limiting development. On the contrary, their goal is rational progress that is beneficial to all parties.

References

Apollo, M. (2015). The clash – Social, environmental and economical changes in tourism destination areas caused by tourism. The case of Himalayan villages (India and Nepal). *Current Issues of Tourism Research, 5*, 6–19.

Apollo, M., & Andreychouk, V. (2021). Mountaineering Adventure tourism and local communities: Social, environmental and economic interactions. Edward Elgar Publishing.

Bui, H. T., Jones, T. E., & Apollo, M. (2021). Reflections for trans-regional mountain tourism. In Jones, T., Bui, H., and Apollo, M. (eds.), Nature-based tourism in Asia's mountainous protected areas (pp. 293–316). Springer.

Craig-Smith, S., & French, C. (1994). *Learning to live with tourism*. Pitman Publishing Pty Limited.

Jodłowski, M. (2010). Postrzeganie sposobów ochrony przyrody i regulacji dotyczących taternictwa powierzchniowego w Tatrzańskim Parku Narodowym przez wspinaczy. In. PTPNoZ, TPN.

Jodłowski, M. (2011). *Zasady dobrej praktyki w zarządzaniu ruchem wspinaczkowym na obszarach chronionych*. Wydawnictwo Uniwersytetu Jagiellońskiego.

Jones, T. E., Apollo, M., & Bui, H. T. (2021). Mountainous protected areas & nature-based tourism in Asia. In Jones, T., Bui, H., and Apollo, M. (eds.), *Nature-based tourism in Asia's mountainous protected areas* (pp. 3–25). Springer.

Kozak, M., & Tasci, A. D. A. (2005). Perceptions of foreign tourists by local service providers: the case of Fethiye, Turkey. *International Journal of Tourism Research, 7*(4–5), 261–277. https://doi.org/10.1002/jtr.534

Monz, C. (2009). Climbers' attitudes toward recreation resource impacts in The Adirondack Park's Giant Mountain Wilderness. *International Journal of Wilderness, 14*(1), 26–26.

Nettekoven, L. (1972). *Massentourismus in Tunesien*. Studienkreis für Tourismus und Entwicklung e.V.

Przecławski, K. (1997). *Człowiek a turystyka. Zarys socjologii turystyki*. Wydawnictwo Albis.

Pyke, K. & Jodice, P. (2008). *Climbing management: A guide to climbing issues and the development of a climbing management plan*. Access Fund.

Reisinger, Y., & Turner, L. W. (2003). *Cross-cultural behaviour in tourism: Concepts and analysis*. Butterworth-Heinemann.

Waldrup, R., & McEwen, D. (1994). Rockclimbing and wilderness: A study of climbers' attitudes toward wilderness, climbing impacts and regulations. *Trends, 31*(3), 38–42.

Williams, J., & Lawson, R. (2001). Community issues and resident opinions of tourism. *Annals of Tourism Research, 28*(2), 269–290. https://doi.org/10.1016/S0160-7383(00)00030-X

Yun, H. J., & Zhang, X. (2017). Cultural conservation and tourism development in the consolidation stage of the tourism area life cycle model. *Tourism Planning and Development, 14*(3), 353–368. https://doi.org/10.1080/21568316.2016.1243147

6   Conclusion and future outlook

Abstract:

In the final section, we revisit the key points of this book. We conceptualise mountaineering in tourism research by capturing the core concepts, examples, and theories from this book and provide an outlook on the areas for future research. The book concludes that the holistic approach proposed by Apollo and Andreychouk should dominate the development of management plans for mountain areas in the future. Otherwise, sustainable development will never be achieved in mountainous areas where different interest groups intertwine.

Mountains are an essential resource for our planet; they provide 60–80 per cent of all fresh water in the world, they are repositories of unique biodiversity, and they are home to 15 per cent of the world's population (more than 90 per cent of which resides in developing regions). Mountains are both important religious locations that attract millions of pilgrims each year and places for recreation and tourism. The popularisation of adventure tourism and commodification of mountaineering over the past three decades have led to the development of mass mountaineering tourism, often located in the most distant and less developed mountain regions characterised by diverse ethnic cultures and traditions. Despite this development, impoverished and isolated mountainous regions are vulnerable to outside influences, climate change, and natural hazards and lack opportunities for development, especially for young people. The negative impacts of, and challenges associated with, fulfilling UN Sustainable Development Goals are pressing issues in mountainous areas, highlighting the urgent need to increase the resilience of people and ecosystems in these areas (Food and Agriculture Organization, 2016). Hence, the development of tourism in mountain areas should align with

DOI: 10.4324/9781003095323-6

the conservation of mountain ecosystems and involve local communities not only as service providers but also as communities in policy planning to ensure long-term sustainable development in line with the UN Sustainable Development Goals.

Human activity in the mountains and mountaineering tourism have been looked at from the perspective of various academic disciplines; hence, the terminology varies. This book draws on interdisciplinary work to provide the essential knowledge on mountaineering tourism and disentangle the overlapping terms and definitions. Considering the recent developments in mountaineering and the commodification of mountaineering tourism, the boundaries between 'elite' mountaineering and tourism have blurred. We see mountaineering tourism as part of adventure tourism and a subset of mountain tourism (any tourism activity in a mountain environment, including fishing, skiing, and paragliding; Apollo & Wengel, 2022).

Following the research by Apollo (2021), we propose to subdivide mountaineering into three categories: (1) climbing (which now refers to adventure climbing or sports climbing), (2) trekking, and (3) hiking (hill-walking in the mountains). Furthermore, we identify six key stages over the last 250 years: (1) pre-mountaineering (until 1786), (2) early mountaineering (1786–1864), (3) classic mountaineering (1864–1899), (4) modern mountaineering (1900–1964), (5) contemporary mountaineering (1964–2021), and (6) commercial mass mountaineering (2021 onwards).

Early encounters with mountains were mainly related to religious rituals or exploration of new lands, whereas the pre-mountaineering period was marked by the great geographical discoveries in the high mountains. The ascent of Mont Blanc in 1786 gave birth to mountaineering in the contemporary sense. The following periods, classic and modern mountaineering, were highlighted by active exploration of European and Asian high-altitude mountains, mainly dominated by European and American mountaineers. The contemporary mountaineering period saw the transition of mountaineering from an 'elite' activity to a mass-commodified form of recreation. This period was marked by several outstanding events, including the first oxygen-free solo ascent of Everest (by Reinhold Messner) and the creation of the Seven Summits Challenge, with the aim of reaching the highest peak on every continent (Richard Brass being the first person to do so). Alex Honnold free-solo[1]-climbed the Freerider route on El Capitan, and Nirmal Purja conquered the world's 14 highest peaks in 189 days. We propose that the recent and perhaps most technically challenging winter ascent of K2 by a team of Nepali mountaineers has set the stage for the new period of commercial mass mountaineering.

Chapter 2 provides an overview of the divisions and types of mountaineering. Overall, mountaineering is comprised of hiking, trekking, and mountain climbing, and each of these activities can have an organised form (when a trekking company organises a trip) and an unorganised form (Kiełkowska & Kiełkowski, 2003; Apollo, 2017). Furthermore, we point out that mountaineering activity can be divided by the (1) climbing season (summer and winter mountaineering), (2) climbing techniques (traditional climbing and climbing with supplementary tools), and (3) type of ground, subdivided into rock, ice, snow, and mixed climbing, which requires both rock- and ice-climbing techniques (see, for example, Eng, 2010; Hattingh, 2000; Kiełkowska & Kiełkowski, 2003). The true accessibility of mountaineering is discussed, and, finally, the chapter considers meteorology in the mountains and the human body in the high-altitude environment.

Chapter 3 talks about mountaineering as a tourism experience and provides a historical overview. The chapter classifies contemporary mountaineers into three distinct categories – (1) true mountaineers, (2) recreational mountaineers, and (3) novice mountaineers – and describes each category in detail. The chapter concludes with a discussion on the personal impacts of mountaineering and touches on ethics and codes of conduct used by mountaineers. Chapter 4 focuses on the impacts of mountaineering, and Chapter 5 discusses the management practices in mountain regions.

For the first time in mountaineering tourism literature, this book attempts to summarise various overlapping definitions relevant to the field and provides the foundation for several terms, including 'mountaineering' itself. As such, in many countries, generic terms exist for all mountain activities, including various forms of tourism and mountaineering, as well as operational, scientific, and other activities. While in English-speaking countries the term is 'mountaineering', in German-speaking countries it is 'Bergsteigen' and in Spanish-speaking countries the word 'montañismo' is used. Unfortunately, these concepts are not only not identical in different languages but often even contradictory (see, for example, 'mountaineering' in Pomfret [2006]; 'Bergsteigen' in Grupp [2008]; 'montañismo' in Osorio [2016]). For this reason, the term is now often redefined (Apollo, 2017b; Beedie & Hudson, 2003). Therefore, in this book, we aimed to bring clarity to the terms because we see it as an essential step if we are to move from the existing challenges related to the management of mountaineering tourism.

Second, we bring attention to some forgotten issues (gaps) in the mountaineering literature, such as the true accessibility of mountaineering (Apollo, 2017b; Apollo & Rettinger, 2019), human waste (Apollo, 2017a), the balances in the high-mountain environment (Apollo & Andreychouk, 2022), and the new host–guest reciprocity at altitude (Apollo et al., 2020). Furthermore, we propose that contemporary mountaineers be classified into the following three categories: true mountaineers, recreational mountaineers, and novice mountaineers. Each of these distinct groups has their own behaviours and consumption patterns of mountaineering as a tourism experience. At the time of writing of this book, during the global pandemic, Covid-19 cases are still on the rise in some countries. No altitude is too high for Covid-19 – a climber at the Everest Base Camp was initially thought to have high-altitude pulmonary edema but actually tested positive for Covid-19 at the hospital in Kathmandu; the rest of their expedition team then began quarantine at the base camp, 5,380 m above sea level (Gee, 2021). In this book, we attempt to bridge the gaps mentioned above by explaining the issues linked to contemporary mountaineering tourism in greater detail as well as providing some recommendations and management implications.

Third, this book incorporates our personal extensive mountaineering experience. We organised independent expeditions in high-altitude mountain environments and conducted data collection at levels as high as 7,000 m above sea level. As professional mountaineers, expedition leaders, and outdoor instructors, we have climbed many high-altitude peaks, and we embrace the traditional unwritten mountaineering 'code of conduct'. Thus, this book is written by both academics and professional mountaineers, who have achieved in the field of alpinism, including the first ascent on virgin peaks in the Lahaul Himalayas (Apollo, 2013). As mountaineers, researchers, and educators, we genuinely care about mountain regions and the people living in them. In this book, we address some of the existing challenges and suggest sustainable policy recommendations for well-visited mountain destinations.

The presented management plan model (see Figure 5.1), both in its descriptive and graphic forms, can provide substantive support for people preparing plans for the protection of nature in high-mountain areas. Due to the number of connections and interdependencies between individual elements of the natural and socioeconomic environment (presented in each chapter), it is only through care for the protection of each element that we will bring the desired effect: minimising the negative impact of mountaineering (hiking, trekking, and mountain climbing). Thus, the holistic approach proposed by Apollo and Andreychouk (2020) should dominate the development of such plans for the future. Otherwise, sustainable development will never be achieved in mountainous areas where different interest groups intertwine.

As mountaineering tourism research progresses, we recommended a focus on the interplay of climate change, conservation, and integrated management policies that aim to contribute to the sustainable development of mountain communities.

Note

1 Free solo climbing (or free soloing) refers to form of climbing in which a climber does not use technical aids and safety equipment (including ropes, harnesses, carabiners etc.).

References

Apollo, M. (2013). Miyar Valley. *American Alpine Journal, 87*(55), 310–311.

Apollo, M. (2017a). The good, the bad and the ugly – Three approaches to management of human waste in a high-mountain environment. *International Journal of Environmental Studies, 74*(1), 129–158. https://doi.org/10. 1080/00207233.2016.1227225

Apollo, M. (2017b). The true accessibility of mountaineering: The case of the High Himalaya. *Journal of Outdoor Recreation and Tourism, 17*, 29–43. https://doi.org/10.1016/j.jort.2016.12.001

Apollo, M. (2021). *Environmental impacts of mountaineering: A conceptual framework*. Springer.

Apollo, M., & Andreychouk, V. (2020). Mountaineering and the natural environment in developing countries: An insight to a comprehensive approach. *International Journal of Environmental Studies*, 1–12. https://doi.org/10. 1080/00207233.2019.1704047

Apollo, M., & Andreychouk, V. (2022). *Mountaineering adventure tourism and local communities: Social, environmental and economic interactions, 77(6)*, 942–953. Edward Elgar Publishing.

Apollo, M., Andreychouk, V., Moolio, P., Wengel, Y., & Myga-Piątek, U. (2020). Does the altitude of habitat influence residents' attitudes to guests? A new dimension in the residents' attitudes to tourism. *Journal of Outdoor Recreation and Tourism, 31*, 100312. https://doi.org/10.1016/j.jort.2020.100312

Apollo, M., & Rettinger, R. (2019). Mountaineering in Cuba: Improvement of true accessibility as an opportunity for regional development of communities outside the tourism enclaves. *Current Issues in Tourism, 15*(22), 1797–1804. https://doi.org/10.1080/13683500.2018.1446920

Apollo, M., & Wengel, Y. (2022). Mountaineering tourism. In D. Buhalis (Ed.), *Encyclopaedia of tourism management and marketing*. Edward Elgar Publishing Limited.

Beedie, P., & Hudson, S. (2003). Emergence of mountain-based adventure tourism. *Annals of Tourism Research, 30*(3), 625–643. https://doi.org/10.1016/ S0160-7383(03)00043-4

Eng, R. C. (2010). *Mountaineering: The Freedom of the Hills.* Mountaineers Books.

Food and Agriculture Organization. (2016). *Working together for mountain peoples and environments.* FAO.

Gee, T. (2021). The first case of COVID-19 at Everest Base Camp. Outside. *Outside Magazine* (Online). Retrieved April 20 2021 from https://www. outsideonline.com/2422521/first-case-covid-19-everest-base-camp

Grupp, P. (2008). *Faszination Berg: die Geschichte des Alpinismus.* Böhlau Verlag.

Hattingh, G. (2000). *The climber's handbook.* New Holland Publishing.

Kiełkowska, M., & Kiełkowski, J. (Eds.). (2003). *Wielka encyklopedia gór i alpinizmu.* Wydawnictwo Stapis.

Osorio, J. A. O. (2016). La aventura del turismo; revivificando la cultura a través del turismo y el patrimonio. *International Journal of Scientific Management and Tourism, 2*(2), 285–295.

Pomfret, G. (2006). Mountaineering adventure tourists: A conceptual framework for research. *Tourism Management, 27*(1), 113–123. https://doi. org/10.1016/j.tourman.2004.08.003

Index